The Writing Workshop Teacher's Guide to Multimodal Composition (K–5)

Multimodal composition is a meaningful and critical way for students to tell their stories, make good arguments, and share their expertise in today's world. In this helpful resource, writer, teacher, and best-selling author Angela Stockman illustrates the importance of making writing a multimodal endeavor in K–5 workshops by providing peeks into the classrooms she teaches within. Chapters address what multimodal composition is, how to situate it in a writing workshop that is responsive to the unique needs of writers, how to handle curriculum design and assessment, and how to plan instruction. The appendices offer tangible tools and resources that will help you implement and sustain this work in your own classroom. Ideal for teachers of grades K–5, literacy coaches, and curriculum leaders, this book will help you and your students reimagine what a workshop can be when the writers within it produce far more than written words.

Angela Stockman is an Instructional Designer who also teaches in the Education and Hybrid Liberal Studies programs at Daemen College in Amherst, New York. The author of *Creating Inclusive Writing Environments in the K–12 Classroom: Reluctance, Resistance, and Strategies that Make a Difference* (2021), Angela is regularly invited to lead curriculum and assessment design work in K–12 schools, where she also conducts lesson studies upon request. You may find her on Twitter at @AngelaStockman or on Instagram @Angela_MakeWriting. She also blogs at www.angelastockman.com.

**Also Available from Routledge
Eye On Education**
www.routledge.com/K-12

**The Writing Workshop Teacher's Guide to
Multimodal Composition (6–12)**
Angela Stockman

**Creating Inclusive Writing Environments
in the K–12 Classroom:
Reluctance, Resistance, and Strategies
that Make a Difference**
Angela Stockman

**Identity-Affirming Classrooms:
Spaces that Center Humanity**
Erica Buchanan-Rivera

**Passionate Readers:
The Art of Reaching and Engaging Every Child**
Pernille Ripp

**Passionate Learners, 2e:
How to Engage and Empower Your Students**
Pernille Ripp

**The Elementary School Grammar Toolkit:
Using Mentor Texts to Teach Standards-Based
Language and Grammar in Grades 3–5**
Sean Ruday

Support Material

The appendices from the book are available on the Routledge website as free downloads. Additional appendix materials are available online only on the author's website.

To access Andrea Schaber's Story; Feedback Structures, Protocols, and Frames for Writers and Designers; Five Ways to Explore Identity with Young Writers and Designers; Mentor Text Sources and Tools for Young Writers and Designers; Multimodal Mentor Texts; Publishing Opportunities for Young Writers; and Starter Sets, please visit the book product page: www.routledge.com/9781032078267. Click on the tab that says "Support Material" and select the files. They will begin downloading to your computer.

To access Multimodal Composition: The Planning Tools; Talking with Writers and Designers; Documenting Progress Toward Learning Targets; Studying Learning; and Using the ACT Model to Plan, please visit the author link: https://angelastockman.com/resources-2/.

The Writing Workshop Teacher's Guide to Multimodal Composition (K–5)

Angela Stockman

Taylor & Francis Group
NEW YORK AND LONDON

Cover image: © Getty Images

First published 2023
by Routledge
605 Third Avenue, New York, NY 10158

and by Routledge
4 Park Square, Milton Park, Abingdon, Oxon, OX14 4RN

Routledge is an imprint of the Taylor & Francis Group, an informa business

© 2023 Angela Stockman

The right of Angela Stockman to be identified as author of this work has been asserted in accordance with sections 77 and 78 of the Copyright, Designs and Patents Act 1988.

All rights reserved. The purchase of this copyright material confers the right on the purchasing institution to photocopy or download pages which bear the copyright line at the bottom of the page. No other parts of this book may be reprinted or reproduced or utilised in any form or by any electronic, mechanical, or other means, now known or hereafter invented, including photocopying and recording, or in any information storage or retrieval system, without permission in writing from the publishers.

Trademark notice: Product or corporate names may be trademarks or registered trademarks, and are used only for identification and explanation without intent to infringe.

Library of Congress Cataloging-in-Publication Data
Names: Stockman, Angela, author.
Title: The writing workshop teacher's guide to multimodal composition (K-5) / Angela Stockman.
Description: New York, NY: Routledge, 2023. | Series: Routledge eye on education | Includes bibliographical references. | Identifiers: LCCN 2022013628 (print) | LCCN 2022013629 (ebook) | ISBN 9781032107660 (hardback) | ISBN 9781032078267 (paperback) | ISBN 9781003216940 (ebook)
Subjects: LCSH: English language—Composition and exercises—Study and teaching (Elementary) | Composition (Language arts)—Study and teaching (Elementary) | Writers' workshops.
Classification: LCC LB1576 .S79884 2023 (print) | LCC LB1576 (ebook) | DDC 372.62/3044—dc23/eng/20220521
LC record available at https://lccn.loc.gov/2022013628
LC ebook record available at https://lccn.loc.gov/2022013629

ISBN: 978-1-032-10766-0 (hbk)
ISBN: 978-1-032-07826-7 (pbk)
ISBN: 978-1-003-21694-0 (ebk)

DOI: 10.4324/9781003216940

Typeset in Palatino
by Apex CoVantage, LLC

Access the Support Material: www.routledge.com/9781032078267

Table of Contents

Preface   *x*

Introduction: Why It's Time for Workshop to Go Multimodal   1
What's Print Privilege?   1
Why Do We Do This?   2
It Begins With You   6
Who I Learn From   7
How This Book Is Organized   7
My Intended Audience   8
Who Am I?   8

Part 1: What Is Multimodal Composition?   9

1 What's Multimodal Composition?   11
Defining Multimodal Composition   12
Compositions—and Humans—Made Whole   16
Workshop Is Everlasting   19
Sixty Second Reflection   20

2 The Multimodal Writing Workshop   21
A Peek into a Make Writing Studio   22
Familiar Territory   25
Essential Workshop Elements that Stand the Test of Time   25
So, What Makes a Multimodal Writing Workshop Different?   26
Four Ways to Situate Multimodal Composition Inside
   of Your Current Writing Workshop   28
Begin with Identity Work   29
A Peek Inside a Make Writing Studio Session   29
Grow Your Curricular Toolkit   31
Prepare to Document Your Learning, and Invite
   Writers to Do the Same   34
Confer with Careful Intention   35
Sixty Second Reflection   38

Part 2: How Do We Create Multimodal Writing Workshops?   41

3   A Blueprint for the Multimodal Writing Workshop   43
    Learning the Language of Leaves   44
    Defining Your Workshop's Load-bearing Walls   45
    Creating Learning Experiences that Deepen Self-Awareness   47
    Building Trusting Relationships   52
    A Peek Inside My Practice   54
    Creating an Environment that Sustains Diverse Writers
       Through Diverse Processes   55
    Instructional Support that Prepares Writers to Produce
       Real Things for Real Audiences that Appreciate Them   57
    Sixty Second Reflection   60

4   Curriculum Design   62
    Defining the Ways We Create Curriculum   64
    The Essential Elements of a High Quality Curriculum
       Design Experience   66
    ACT: The Learning for Transfer Mental Model   67
    Situating Standards Within the Frame   71
    Hanging It All Together   72
    Sixty Second Reflection   75

5   Assessing Multimodal Processes and Products   76
    Curriculum, Assessment, and Instruction Work Hand-in-Hand   77
    A Peek into My Documentation Process   79
    Documenting to Do Less Harm   80
    Grading and Reporting   82
    And What About Report Cards?   83
    Framing Better Feedback   84
    Sixty Second Reflection   85

Part 3: How Do We Teach Multimodal Composition?   87

**6   Mentor Texts, Planning, and the Essential Elements of a
    Multimodal Composition**   89
    The Essential Elements of a Multimodal Composition   91
    Analyzing Multimodal Mentor Texts   97
    Differentiated Investigations of a Form   98
    The Designer's Notebook   101
    How Experienced Writers and Designers Build Prototypes   104

Making the Writing Process Multimodal for
   Inexperienced Writers   105
Sixty Second Reflection   106

7 Pitches, Prototypes, and Feedback   **107**
Emphasis   108
Contrast   110
Color   110
Organization   111
Alignment   112
Proximity   112
Considering Design Choices in Mentor Texts   113
Pitching to Peer Review   114
Sixty Second Reflection   117

**8 Launching a Multimodal Composition
into the World**   **118**
Helping Our Youngest Writers Create Things for
   Authentic Purposes   119
Helping More Experienced Writers and Designers
   Launch Their Work   121
Timing the Launch   122
Reflecting to Learn   125
Publication Outlets for Writers of All Ages   126
Sixty Second Reflection   126

Appendix A: Planning Tools   **129**
Andrea Schaber's Story   131
Feedback Structures, Protocols, and Frames for
   Writers and Designers   140
Five Ways to Explore Identity with Young
   Writers and Designers   144

Appendix B: Tools for Writers   **147**
Mentor Text Sources and Tools for Young Writers and Designers   149
Multimodal Mentor Texts   157
Publishing Opportunities for Young Writers and Designers   161
Starter Sets   162

Preface

I go to school. My baby sister doesn't, but I do, and my teacher likes to read us stories. Every day, we all curl up on the carpet after lunch. She reads to us while Kevin Clark sits in front of me and picks his nose and eats it and eventually falls asleep. I like Kevin okay, but I won't hold his hand in line because of the boogers.

Pinchy-face Patty sits in a desk right next to mine. She wears a different white sweater over her uniform every single day, and her lunch box is plaid with a shiny black handle. She wears her hair in a big white bow, and her socks have tiny roses at the knee. Her mom is a professor. Mine does hair. I don't know how she knows this about my mom, but she makes sure that I know that she knows this every single day. She rolls her eyes when she reminds me, too. I cross my eyes and curl my tongue back at her. That's a special skill, my dad told me. Not everyone can roll their tongue and cross their eyes. I tell Patty this, and she tries to do it, too, but she can't. This makes her face get extra pinchy.

Patty tells us to shush when we line up for lunch, and she is always first to raise her hand. Her mom volunteers at our school, and she says that this makes her the boss. Her mom's face isn't pinchy, though. It's actually very pretty, and when she talks with us, her voice gets so high that even her own eyes widen in surprise. I like her.

Patty had a birthday party at the roller rink and a sleep over at her house right after. Her parents had just painted the living room, and that's where we were sleeping. "On the new Ethan Allen!" her pretty-faced professor mom exclaimed, her eyes opening so far they nearly swallowed her entire face. I could not wait to sleep on that furniture.

But the paint fumes made me dizzy and then queasy and then sick. While the other girls played pin the tail on the donkey, I pushed my face deep into the cushions of Patty's brand new couch. Breathing in and breathing out, I tried to make my head stop spinning. Then, I coughed up cake and ice cream and what was left of my pizza.

When Mom came to pick me up, pinchy-face Patty just had to show her my mess. "That couch is ruined forever now," she said. "Our brand new couch. Ruined."

Mom apologized and offered to have it cleaned, but Patty's mom said no dear and it's okay and what matters is that Angie gets well.

"Come on," Mom said as she picked up my bag. "Let's get you home."

"Angie vomited on our couch," I heard Patty whisper to the other girls in the coat room on Monday morning. "My party was ruined. In fact, my entire house was ruined. It smelled like puke for days."

"Shhhhh!" I hushed her, just the way she always hushed me, and Kevin Clark started laughing because no one ever shushed pinchy-face Patty. She started fake crying like she always does—and I almost high-fived him—but then I remembered the boogers, and I quickly yanked my hand back.

"Angie!" My teacher yelled when she saw Patty's tears and Kevin's broken eyes. "Why on earth would you do such a thing? Kevin you may take Patty's hand in line today, and Angie, you may walk alone."

I covered my smile with my booger-free hand as we took our places in line and headed down the hall, toward the art room. I wondered if Patty's fingers were sticky yet, and this made me smile. Because I'm mean on the inside sometimes, that's why.

Mrs. Scott never seemed to care about that, though. She was my kindergarten teacher, and she still waved at me each time we passed her door—her big, bright smile unfurling above the apron she always wore.

"Why?" I asked her one day as she was passing out snacks. Most of the teachers in our school were nuns or teachers who wore dresses and pantyhose and high heels every day. Mrs. Scott wore pastel colored corduroys and penny loafers and her big, messy apron instead.

"Well, learning is a very sloppy thing," she told me, and I nodded because I understood. We used paint and glue and construction paper and glitter almost every day in our classroom. Mrs. Scott crawled around on the floor with us, and she climbed up on ladders to hang our stories from the lights, so everyone could see them. "My pockets are full of the things I need to help you make stuff," she said. "I don't want to have to search for anything. When you need it, you need it, right?" Right! If we needed scissors or a pencil or scented markers or a clip of some kind, Mrs. Scott always had them. She had yarn and watercolors and popsicle sticks in her apron pockets. She had glue sticks and a teeny tiny stapler and rubber bands, too. And those were just the things she carried around in her apron! Our shelves and cupboards were full of lots more.

Mrs. Scott taught us how to write with the sun, making stories and settings out of the shadows it cast. We put on puppet shows and made costumes out of paper bags for the skits we performed on the auditorium stage. She brought us to the play area for show and tell each morning. This is where we learned to share our opinions and where Mrs. Scott used a big chalk board to flip the compositions we were building from blocks and performing for one another into letters and words that were all new to us. Our dress-up box was a writing workshop of its own, although it would be many more years before I fully understood the method behind her magic.

Learning was different in my first grade teacher's classroom. For starters, it was exceptionally tidy. There were no play areas, and the walls were bare, save for one solitary bulletin board that featured ten faded posters: one for each Commandment. I remember this because I spent long days staring into those illustrations, willing the clock to move faster and listening to the laughter through the walls that separated our classroom from Mrs. Scott's.

We weren't allowed to talk much in first grade. This was the rule that seemed to govern everything from the way our curriculum was designed to instruction, assessment, and feedback. When we arrived every morning, pinchy-face Patty herded us into the coat room, ordered the removal of our book bags and jackets, and then escorted us in a single, silent line to our desks, where we each had our own little stack of workbooks. The important page numbers were listed on the chalkboard, and we looked up at them and then, down. Then, we used our pencils to fill out the pages. Our teacher didn't talk to us unless she was correcting us. I don't remember her face or even her name, but I do remember the tone of her voice and how my shoulders tightened each time she wandered past my desk to point out where my penmanship was lacking.

"Letters and words and numbers are what matter most in first grade," she reminded me. "You're not a baby anymore. You need to write better."

And I did. Now that I think about it, writing was the only mode of communication that seemed to be of value that year. If we were to be heard at all, we needed to use letters and words correctly.

It was no wonder that by fourth grade, I was filling tablets with long lines of notes that my teacher strung across multiple chalkboards. I wrote my first research paper on Maria Tallchief that year. I remember nothing about the pages I produced, but I do remember spending hours sprawled across my cold basement floor sketching my subject into a perfect tenth position for my cover. I was proud of the illustration that emerged, many erasures later. Her face showed exactly what I wanted it to—exactly what I didn't have words for just yet.

"Can I draw the rest of this report?" I'd asked my teacher, knowing what the answer would be.

"Drawing doesn't count," she told me. "You're a big girl. You need to write."

And so I did.

I wrote my way through elementary school, junior and senior high, and college. I wrote my way through my teaching certification exams, and then, toward the front of the first classroom where I taught other elementary school students about the importance of letters and words. I was the first in my family to go to college, and shortly after I began teaching, I was the first to finish graduate school, too.

"So now you're a writing teacher," my Grandpa Jim smiled at me one afternoon, a moment after I'd earned my Master's Degree. It was as if he were noticing this for the very first time. I nodded, uncertain of his purposes and admittedly, a bit self-conscious about that accomplishment. In my family, academic pedigree meant little. Hard, physical work was what mattered.

When my father met my favorite English professor at my college graduation, he said, "I know that guy has written a bunch of stuff, but I felt the calluses on his hand when I shook it. They impressed me more."

And I knew that they would.

This was the same year that my grandmother was diagnosed with cancer. She died shortly after my graduation, leaving Grandpa Jim with little more than his stories. "Do you think you might write them for me?" he asked. "I'm not sure how to put them down on paper myself. I want to leave something of myself behind, though."

I was so humbled by this request that I could not reply, but that was okay. Grandpa Jim did all of the talking, and I was an attentive listener. I learned that my grandfather lived a storied existence that was much different from my own. His first wife was Native American. They raised their children on the Tuscarora Reservation, and the reservation, he said, raised him. He married my grandmother—the white woman who became his second wife—late in life. It was her second marriage as well. Her own children were grown, and her husband, the grandfather I never met, passed away just before I was born. He owned a hobby shop and was a maker himself. Although I never knew him, I like to think I inherited a bit of his creative DNA.

When I was just a baby, Grandpa Jim built my grandmother a five bedroom log cabin, a great big barn, and a woodworking shop on a few acres of land near the reservation. He did this with his own two hands, a circle of friends, and a pair of divining rods that helped them find the water lines. There, he became the grandfather I knew and loved: a farmer who taught me how to gather eggs from the chicken coup, a woodworker who made my own daughter's first rocking horse, and a storyteller who helped me feel less alone inside of a family that had little appreciation for nature, spirituality, or the perfect tenderness of their own human hearts.

During the last few years of his life, Grandpa Jim told his stories to me, and I did my best to transcribe them. His stories would be his legacy, he said, and I was helping him create them. But even then, I knew that my feeble letters and words were far too primitive for such a significant task. When the writing was done, I left the pages with him. I don't know where they are—or even *if* they are—today. It doesn't matter. All of these years later, my grandfather's stories weave their way through so many of my days.

I remember him every time a rooster crows or I hear a baby goat bleating. I see him in the steely autumn sky that hangs above the fields he once hunted and in the cranberry and popcorn strings I tuck into our Christmas tree branches each year. Grandpa Jim wanders the aisles with me every time I visit the antique stores near his cabin. I see him in the tools and the materials I find there. I still can't make a pumpkin pie without remembering the stringy ones he tried—and failed—to make from scratch each year. They were horrible and wonderful, and I'm so glad he knew that stories were made with so much more than mere written words.

Grandpa Jim knew that living, playing, and making were writing. These were not childish indulgences but in fact, essential elements of his very rich writerly life. He may have known that I could help him find words, and at one point, he thought he needed them in order to ensure that his life transcended his death. I also believe that he knew, in the end, that those written words would fail us both. His life was bigger than print.

So often, primary and elementary teachers are led to believe that making is something we engage young writers with temporarily and move them through in order to inspire the production of print. Grandpa Jim taught me that in the absence of sight, sound, scent, and vibration, there is no story or lesson or argument to be made.

Making is writing, and we write across the landscape of every one of our days, whether we know we're doing that or not. Our lives are our legacies, and when we invite others to share them, we build stories together that even death cannot dismantle. My grandfather taught me that it's only in solitude that writing ceases to exist. When we invite company around us and take care to communicate with them, we are writers, no matter our mode.

I hope this book reminds you of all that you already do to serve young writers and designers well. I hope it inspires you to make your writing workshops spaces where they learn to notice, tinker, and linger with materials, moments, and the space itself and not just their written words. I hope these experiences sustain them as they tumble toward adolescence and into adulthood, too. I hope this book fills your apron pockets. Most importantly, I hope your students remember your name, your voice, and your legacy.

Introduction

Why It's Time for Workshop to Go Multimodal

In 2015, I published a little book called *Make Writing: 5 Teaching Strategies that Turn Writer's Workshop into a Makerspace.* This was the story of how my students were disrupting everything I thought I knew about how to teach writing well. There, readers met makers like Luke, the kindergarten student who built complex narratives from LEGO and ran tech playgrounds for teachers despite the concerns that so many like me maintained about his "resistance" to writing. That first book was a reflection of my early learning about the relationship between making and writing, and it helped me find what I know has become my lifelong work in the field. Seven years later, I remain humbled by young writers and designers like Luke. I know a bit more about what writing really is and how we might teach it better, too—if we're willing to check our print privilege a bit.

What's Print Privilege?

We privilege print when we value it more than every other legitimate mode of expression. When we require the use of written words in any setting, we're privileging print. When we demand them on high stakes assessments of standards that have nothing to do with the mastery of written expression, we allow our print privilege to foster deep and destructive inequities.

Is it important for young people to develop a facility for written words? Of course it is. Is alphabetic expression the most important mode of communication, though? It's not, and yet, we center the production of print in all of our writing workshop endeavors, making the use of materials and other modalities peripheral to that singular purpose.

Why Do We Do This?

That's an essential question that I'll likely spend the rest of my lifetime pursuing, but there are few theories I tend to maintain here. Suppositions, if you will:

- Writing workshop was still in its infancy when many of us encountered it. When we encountered it, it changed our lives. When it changed our lives, we fell in love with that single story of what a writing workshop was and how to establish and sustain one well. Print was the main character in that story that we know and love so well. And nostalgia and love are powerful things.
- We've learned much more about writing workshop over time, but we've rarely applied the critical lenses that our cultural and racial histories provide us to any of that learning. Our workshops remain rooted in whiteness and print privilege as a result. We've only begun to interrogate that reality collectively, and too many are resistant to that work.
- Discussions of multimodality tend to perseverate on digital writing and the tools that support it, leaving those who are not tech comfortable struggling to lead learning inside of today's connected learning spaces. This misperception often leaves those who are tech comfortable with a limited definition of what multimodality truly is as well.
- Poorly executed standards and reform movements perpetuated harmful definitions of what writing is, what kinds of writing matter, and what makes a writer successful.

When champions of multimodal composition like myself begin knocking on workshop doors and finding ourselves invited in, we're often greeted by creative and committed teachers who are the first to reveal how daunting it is to be called to teach writing, how little time they have to pursue their own creative projects, and how worried they are about whatever test the writers they know and love will find themselves subjected to in the near future. Tests tend to define writing as the production of written words. Far too often, tests also inspires what—and how—teachers will teach and learn.

How often do you infuse writing instruction with opportunities to read, listen, speak, tinker, and play with creative materials using modes other than written words? If you're like most K–5 writing teachers I know, you're always designing learning experiences like these. How often is all of that reading, speaking, tinkering, and play done largely in service to the production of written words in your writing workshop, though? If you're like most K–5 writing teachers I know, you're likely framing play as a way to inspire or even finesse children into more serious academic work and writing, and if you're not, you may be feeling like you're failing.

I meet some teachers who are passionate about their own professional learning. They thrive inside of the uncertainty. Teaching is a life-long experiment, and they're always amazed by their findings. I meet many more who are so worried about performance and all that it's tied to that they are unable to invest in their own rich and wide professional learning. They struggle to teach to their fullest potential, as a result. They feel this, too. It weighs on them.

When I step across any workshop threshold, I also greet handfuls of writers who share my affinity for the written word but a bunch more who claim to prefer to MAKE compositions instead. Their teachers often refer to the former group as gifted and the latter group as reluctant, resistant, or worse, struggling. I still catch myself doing the same once in a while. I have no virtue to signal here. In fact, it's important that I come to this conversation with you honestly. I noticed the influence of making on writers and their processes only because I was trying to solve a problem I'd defined, and that problem was resistance to writing. Making was a solution for those who seemed to struggle with the written word.

I had to research and write three more books before I realized how problematic some of my thinking and many of my adopted "best" practices were.

Context matters, and many writing teachers, including myself, have missed quite a bit of it as we came up in this profession. We completed teaching certification experiences that never exposed us to cultural differences, the way print came to be privileged in our classrooms, who schools were designed by, and most important—who they were designed for.

Few writing teachers raise their hands when I ask them if they were required to take more than one linguistics course in undergraduate or graduate school, if they ever made a study of anthropology, or if they know much about how our cultural and racial histories may have shaped the way writing workshop came to be defined and even—branded—in our profession.

Those who embrace multimodal composition typically came to it through art, or more often, their enthusiasm for digital writing. These are powerful entry points, but multimodal composition is bigger than both of those things combined. All expression is multimodal in nature, and all of it is influenced by our identities as well.

Sadly, when we speak about multimodal composition, we tend to emphasize the art and science of composition while taking the composer for granted. Sure, we might speak to their rhetorical or design skills, but we rarely, if ever, connect the assumptions we're making about so-called struggling writers to the fact that we typically define writing as the production of written words alone, and we favor that single form of communication in schools despite the fact that even there, many young writers are very eager and able to express themselves using modes other than print.

The COVID-19 pandemic validated a suspicion I've carried for quite some time: Notions of giftedness or struggle inside of writing workshop are largely defined by how compliant, wealthy, white, and schooled a writer is rather than how nimble, creative, expressive, and worldly they may be. When writers are attentive during mini-lessons, comprehend the mentor texts we provide, apply the strategies we share to achieve the skills we've prioritized, when they produce a reasonable amount of written words that reveal mastery of the conventions we've taught them, we assume they're successful writers. When they embrace the routines and rituals we impose on them, they're successful workshoppers, too. And when they don't do some or all of those things, they're strugglers. Far too often, the teachers who fail to fall in line with these practices are characterized as incompetent as well.

I know this because I led my own workshops this way for many years, and I've spent the last 15 visiting countless others as well. My teacher friends are just as familiar as I am with the scene I've set above, and while most of them are cognizant of the problems inherent in it, they were only just beginning to understand how to resolve those issues when the pandemic pushed all of us out of our workshops and online, where writing and learning have been different experiences that offered unexpected lessons. Many of them were made in the off-hours.

For instance, all of us quickly learned how valuable the connected learners inside of our professional networks are. Having a tech support specialist of any kind on the job inside of our workplaces was a gift, but these people were quickly overwhelmed as they worked to perform rapid remote-learning triage. Many knew they couldn't keep burdening them and instead, turned to their professional learning networks and especially, the connected educators inside of them who knew where to point people, how to design quality remote learning experiences, and how to build and strengthen relationships—virtually.

We also learned that many students who did not shine brightly in our face-to-face workshop spaces were showing up and participating well online. Some were also expressing themselves in ways we did not expect, using tools and approaches that never had a real place inside of our workshops on the ground. They stopped waiting for our invitations, permissions, and perfectly crafted demonstrations and instead, used the tools they had at their disposal to make unexpected and delightful things. Many students became our mentors, and they also gained newfound confidence in themselves as learners and creators and contributors, too.

On a personal level, I noted that some of the students I'd previously defined as gifted writers in my own classroom or Studio struggled inside of professional roles that were suddenly demanding the use of design skills they'd never acquainted themselves with. I also noticed how some of the writers I'd previously worried about were the ones who shifted quickly, responding to new and unexpected work demands and opportunities with agility, if not ease. They were excited to use new tools, try new approaches, and tinker with different modes of expression. They were also the first to walk away from professional circumstances that were unhealthy and even abusive. They found better jobs or they started their own businesses because they could. Their scrappiness served them well as they learned how to translate forms that didn't play well online into those that did, using the same multimodal composition skills that they developed after school, because their teachers defined that work as non-essential play that wouldn't help them do well on their required assignments and standardized tests.

The fact is that most of the so-called struggling writers I know who are now thriving inside of highly creative spaces didn't land in those positions by happenstance. They came from families and schools and especially—teachers—who had the ability and resources to guide them there.

I've dedicated a good portion of my career to perpetuating this message: Writing is bigger than print, and the world expects something different and so much more from the young writers we serve. While multimodal composition isn't synonymous with digital composition, technology has not only increased opportunities for humans to express themselves using modes other than written words, it's changed how humans prefer to consume messages and information.

Writing teachers like me can't ignore this reality. Until we're explicitly teaching multimodal composition in our classrooms and workshops, we can't honestly claim to be teaching writing—not as it exists in the world today, and not as the world will expect young writers to bring it into existence. We're only teaching the production of written words. And if we're only teaching the production of written words, we're building false confidence in print comfortable writers while silencing talented multimodal composers. There are many of them, and the world is waiting for their arrival.

Industries want writers who know how to turn research findings into gifographics or stop-motion videos or TED Talks. They want writers who know when and how to fold a story into the argument they're making. They need writers who know when to speak and when to listen—and how. It's past time for far more explicit instruction about how context, form, mode, and materials influence message and meaning.

Writers need to know how to design for accessibility. They must have the awareness, skills, and tools to compose for as many diverse users with different interests, needs, and experiences as possible if they're to create influential work that serves the world. Texts must be composed so that readers with limited hearing, sight, or the ability to hold it in their hands may still interact with it.

They must be designed in ways that center historically excluded groups as well. If we understand this, then we understand that it is impossible to accomplish when we privilege print. It's past time for far more intentional, inclusive, and liberatory instruction. Ironically, one of the best ways to accomplish this is to become more aware of multimodal composition in our daily lives, to study its purpose and effect, and use it with greater intention ourselves.

Human beings have always been multimodal composers. Deepening our global, ethical, and accessibility awareness by applying the lens of multimodality to what we consume and create makes it far easier to transform the workshop we've always known and loved into a multimodal writing workshop. The shift feels almost organic when we work on self-awareness first.

It Begins With You

While many conversations about multimodal composition are reserved for middle and high school and university settings, I know that all of these shifts begin with you: primary and intermediate level teachers who need no convincing about the power of play and the influence of image, sound, scent, vibration, culture, and community on learning. I hope you see yourself in the pages that follow, and I hope that you find validation, too. Most importantly, I hope to leave you with a language and lenses that help you teach multimodal composition skills with explicit intention in your K–5 classroom. Everything you do to make learning a multi-sensory and joyful experience for your students is not icing on any cake. It *is* the cake, and your efforts here make it so much richer—sweeter—and more appealing to the audiences that the young writers and designers you serve will ultimately strive to fuel.

Who I Learn From

My work was influenced by the early research of Walter Ong and more recently, the New London Group. Jason Palmeri, Jodie Nicotra, Shawna Coppola, Cheryl Ball, Jennifer Sheppard, and Kristin Arola deepen my understanding of what multimodal composition is and more importantly, how to make this work accessible to young writers. Julie Stern, Kayla Duncan, Krista Ferraro, and Trevor Aleo conceptualized the Learning for Transfer mental model (or ACT model) that carries this work to learners so well. It holds space for my own growth as a teacher. I'm also learning much from scholars such as Dr. Gholdy Muhammad, Zaretta Hammond, Felicia Rose Chavez, and Matthew Salesses.

I've learned much about loose parts play and inviting a multimodal writing process from Lorella Lamonaca and Lindsey Hicks, the founders of a Reggio Emilia study group who welcomed me into the learning community years ago and made space for me on several study tours to the Loris Malaguzzi Centre in Reggio Emilia, Italy. Diane Kashin, Ed.D RECE, has deepened my thinking even further here. I'm grateful to her for sharing such compelling peeks into her own practice and the spaces she creates and inhabits with very young writers and designers.

The fact is that each day uncovers more of my own biases as a writing teacher, the limitations of my education and experiences, and new paths to explore. The pedagogical frames I once relied upon no longer serve me or the students who are most affected by my work as well as I once thought they did. I'm grateful to these wise humans for helping me see and do better.

How This Book Is Organized

This book has four parts, and each builds capacity for the next. The first part is an attempt to demystify multimodal composition and situate it within a K–5 workshop environment. The second speaks to curriculum design and assessment, and the third focuses squarely on instruction. The last part of this book—the appendix (with additional appendix material available at https://angelastockman.com/resources-2/)—includes tangible tools and resources that can help you plan, implement, and sustain this work in your own classroom.

My Intended Audience

I wrote this book for K–5 teachers who are curious about multimodal composition, eager to bring it into their own writing classrooms and workshops, and in need of explicit guidance and tools. If you're unable to imagine what this work might look like, I hope this book offers a clear vision. And if you're ready to try, I hope it guides your planning well.

Who Am I?

I'm currently an Instructional Designer for Daemen College in Amherst, New York. I also teach Advanced Composition and Language in Society within our online hybrid liberal arts program and Assessment Methods in Education and Adolescent Literature inside of our education department. As an independent consultant, I've spent nearly 20 years serving young writers and their teachers in K–12 public, private, and charter schools. I began my career as an elementary school teacher, spent 12 years teaching writing at the middle level, and founded a writing community for children and teachers that is still thriving today. You can find me on Twitter at @AngelaStockman and I'm @angela_makewriting on Instagram. I look forward to meeting you.

Part 1

What Is Multimodal Composition?

1

What's Multimodal Composition?

If you take anything away from this book, I hope it's this bit of validation: The children you teach already have the answers to every question you might ask about writing and how to best teach it. They may not be able to flip a definition of multimodal composition back to you on a dime, but if you study them, they will teach you what it means. This is how they live. It's how they create. Naturally.

Here's my first invitation to you: Put this book aside for a day or even an entire week. Pick up a notebook, a stack of sticky notes, or your phone, and become a documentarian. Follow your students around as they engage with one another. This might happen during your writing workshop or another academic learning block. It might happen on the playground, at the bus stop, or during lunchtime. Where do you see stories? Where do you hear arguments? When do you witness moments where even your youngest learners assume a teaching posture? Try not to draw any conclusions about what you're witnessing—just pay attention, and use whatever tools are most comfortable for you to gather these findings: What do you see? What do you hear?

What does observation teach you about young writers? How does it challenge the assumptions you've made about what writing is and how it's best produced?

Let written words go for just a minute or perhaps, until tomorrow or even next week—even those you find on this page. Come back once you've found a story that's made from much more. There's no need to rush. I'll wait for you.

Defining Multimodal Composition

A multimodal composition is a piece of communication, also known as a text, that is made of different modes, including, but not limited to, print. Modes

WHAT IS MULTIMODAL COMPOSITION?

Multimodal compositions rely on multiple and varied modes of expression in order to communicate messages.

THE SPATIAL MODE

Layout, position, and proximity influence the way the elements of a multimodal design communicate a message. Examples of spatial organization include yearbook and magazine layouts as well as the way panels are organized in comics.

THE GESTURAL MODE

Small body movements, facial expressions, eye movement, and other body language helps us communicate as well. Examples of gestural expression include the way a performer widens her eyes for emphasis as she speaks specific words, the way a puppet hangs his head to reveal grief, and the way an illustrator frames a subject's eyebrows to demonstrate her anger..

THE ALPHABETIC MODE

Many of us have experience using written words to express ourselves. Examples include stories, explanations, and opinions that are composed using letters, words, and conventional spelling, punctuation, mechanics, and grammar.

THE VISUAL MODE

This mode includes the use of images and elements that can be seen. Examples include photography, illustrations, graphics, and emojis.

THE AURAL MODE

Music, ambient noise, sound effects, accents, and tone of voice are all examples of aural expression. The aural mode relies exclusively on sound, and those who design with it take care to consider how what is heard will influence the message.

THE HAPTIC MODE

Touch conveys information. It can also inspire someone to imagine a particular visual. Haptics include the vibrations felt when a smart phone sends a push notification. Some video games rely on haptic expression to communicate information to players through the use of game controllers that vibrate. Braille is haptic, too.

Figure 1.1 What Is Multimodal Composition?

are ways of communicating. We writing teachers tend to have an affinity for the written word, but writing is bigger than this. Writing is spatial, gestural, visual, aural, and haptic, too.

This text will help you explore and then invite young writers to notice and experiment with the interplay between these six modes of expression. When combined with intention, they work together to communicate the whole of a message. Each element in a multimodal composition contributes something to that message that other elements may not.

Experienced writers combine modes and elements for effect, considering how each influences others and how their placement carries or convolutes meaning. Elementary teachers prepare young writers well for this work by bringing multimodal composition into their writing workshops and classrooms with careful intention. Young writers need ample opportunity to explicitly study each mode of expression inside of gorgeous examples and then, tinker, play, and create with them. When such experiences are not the work of a single "special" lesson or unit but instead, fully integrated into the whole of a curriculum, children learn the language of each mode, what all of them share in common, and how they are quite different. More importantly, they learn that writing is far bigger than print and that all of the other modes of expression elevate our capacity for alphabetic expression and the quality of the compositions we create.

That's an important bit of nuance, too: Compositions and texts are not made with written words alone. In fact, they may not be made with written words at all. When I use the terms composition or text in this book and in my work with teachers on the ground, I'm not referring to print alone because multimodal compositions are much more complex. They include but are not limited to street art, dance performances, posters, slam poetry, infographics, theatrical performances, comics, videos, musical compositions, podcasts, sculptures, and memes. If you pay attention, you'll find the seeds of multimodal composition taking root in every K–5 classroom. It happens spontaneously. It's the byproduct of play. Perhaps that's why we take it for granted. Imagine, though, what could happen if we tended this garden with very clear intentions.

Imagine what could happen if we planned to teach multimodal composition explicitly in our writing workshops and classrooms.

What makes a multimodal composition effective is its ability to engage and move those who interact with it. This has much to do with how well the composition addresses a specific rhetorical situation that we are interested in. Successful multimodal composers are keenly aware of their intended audience, the context in which their work will be consumed, and their greater purposes. Analyzing the work of other composers helps us understand the relationship between these factors and how creators attend to them in different ways, for effect (Nicotra, 2019, pp. 2–3). This may not feel like work that your students are capable of, but context is everything. If we have a clear vision of the writer we hope to graduate and the path we hope they'll create along as they move through our school community, we're better able to uncover the trailheads that are waiting for them inside of our own small spaces. For instance, even our youngest and most inexperienced writers are accustomed to studying the work of other authors before they draft their own inside of our writing workshops. Fewer might make a detailed study of design, though.

This book will prepare you to make a much deeper exploration of those concepts with primary and intermediate level writers—chapter by chapter. The tool provided in Figure 1.2 is one that you might use with your own students as you begin to explore examples of multimodal mentor texts for the very first time. You'll find a collection of them in the appendix, if you're seeking meaningful examples.

Bringing multimodal composition into our workshops and classrooms inspires new thinking about the creative process as well. Even when I encounter a text that's made entirely of written words, I struggle to classify it as monomodal now (Shipka, 2011, p. 52). I wonder how many conversations have been had that influence the words on any page. How many multisensory experiences inspired the ideas shared? How much audio, video, or film was consumed as the author conducted research? How many presentations, performances, or other experiences shaped what made it to the page?

In my experience, elementary teachers bring a unique level of awareness to this work. Opportunities for multimodal expression seem to fade as writers age through our school systems. Or at the very least, they become siloed. Let me explain. Elementary teachers intentionally create environments where four- and five- and six- and ten-year-olds engage in purposeful play, and they bear witness to the incredible learning and work that emerges as a result. Many even study this connection.

So, why do our values seem to shift so dramatically as writers enter late elementary school and make their way through the secondary grades? It's easy to blame testing for this, but I struggle to name this as the root cause. Testing, in my opinion, is a symptom of a far more ubiquitous disease. Why do we value testing anyway? What does it offer us? What does it protect? Why does that matter? The answers aren't simple and some may vary from system to system, but grappling with these questions can be quite revealing.

Which brings me to this: Playful learning isn't the domain of primary or intermediate level education alone, and multimodal composition isn't "special." When we treat either of these things as peripheral endeavors—especially as writers grow older—we perpetuate a sort of fragmentation that

ANALYZING A MULTIMODAL COMPOSITION

Questions like these help us appreciate the craft moves made by multimodal composers as they attend to different rhetorical situations.

WHO WAS THIS MADE FOR?

Who did the creator make this for? How do we know? What parts of the piece are proof of this? How does this work speak directly to the specific people who will read, view, listen to, or use this?

HOW DOES THE CREATOR FEEL ABOUT THE TOPIC?

What do we know about the creator? Why did they make this piece? How do they feel about the topic? What is it about this composition that helps us understand this? How do they feel about the form? How do we know?

HOW DOES CONTEXT MATTER?

Where was this composition created? Where was it shared and when? Who is it about? Who is it for? What difference is the creator trying to make? Who will be happy with this? Who will be uncomfortable with it? Who might be hurt by it? How do we know this? Why does that matter? Should we respond? If so, how?

HOW DOES MULTIMODALITY MATTER?

Which modes of expression are used to create this work? How is each mode special? How are modes combined, when, and where? What did the designer seem to do on purpose? How would this work be less meaningful if one of the modes included were removed? How would it be different if we replaced one with another or added another mode entirely?

Figure 1.2 Analyzing a Multimodal Composition

perpetuates deep inequities. Rather than defining writing as anything other than print, we typically invite writers to consume multimodal products in order to provoke the production of letters and words. Or, we push multimodality out of our workshops entirely, deluded by the misperception that drawing, speaking, performing, and building are activities that strong writers move beyond as they begin to place letters and words on pages. We've been led to believe that visual and spatial expression is best taught in art class, that aural composition is the domain of music teachers, and that gestural expression is best taught in the theater. Some tend to assume that multimodal texts are largely digital texts as well.

Compositions—and Humans—Made Whole

These perspectives, while common, inspire us to fracture the whole of the compositional process and attend to disparate modes of expression in disjointed ways. They force writers to compartmentalize and repress elements of their identities and their unique funds of knowledge as well. Outside of the world of academia, writing remains a gloriously multimodal animal that shifts shape in response to human interests, their cultures, their needs, and technological evolution. As our experiences, knowledge, skills, and tools progress, so, too, do opportunities to express ourselves in different ways for different purposes using different media. When writers appreciate the affordances of each different mode of expression, their relationship to one another, and how this collaboration enables a kind of communication that the use of written words alone cannot, they're better able to create works of real influence for audiences that deeply appreciate, and even need them.

This makes your perspective and your practice as a primary and intermediate teacher that much more vital. Everything that you do in service to multimodal expression sharpens your students' compositional saws. The world will require them to produce far more than written words as they enter and try to influence it. These multiple modes of expression are not developmental tools that writers should be encouraged to abandon in service to the production of high volumes of print as children grow. They enable all influential writers to compose work that is worthy of the world inside of a process that is worthy of their participation.

The multimodal compositional process is one that invites writers to understand and engage with the whole of who they are, including their racial and cultural histories, experiences, and the expressive modes and tools they've become adept at using within, and more likely beyond, their schools. Young children do this naturally, until they're discouraged from doing so. We sacrifice much in service to what does not matter and what will not serve us well in return.

Our world is culturally and linguistically diverse. It's also increasingly globalized. Information and multimedia technologies foster the development of far more dynamic text forms than we typically encounter in our writing classrooms and workshops. Beyond the boundaries of those spaces, multitudes of multicultural humans rely on these tools to communicate and learn together across distance and time, inclusively. These same technologies also invite great disparity where access is denied. Many are all too familiar with the learning barriers created by this reality—especially writing teachers who work within systems that privilege the production of written words in the form of five paragraph essays and common literature reviews. The liberatory nature of multimodal composition empowers humans of all ages and from every walk of life to create to their very fullest potential, influencing audiences where they live, using just-right modes and means of expression (The New London Group, 1996, pp. 60–61).

It took a long time for me to understand my power and my responsibilities as a writing teacher and a consultant who serves other writers and their teachers. Workshops that do not make space for multimodal composition produce writers, work, and entire worlds that long for completion. Our histories, cultures, purposes, processes, and tools will continue to change, and new modes of expression may even reveal themselves over time as well, but these understandings might serve as a foundation for quality writing workshops that serve multimodal composers of all ages (Arola et al., 2018, p. 6). This is how you might contextualize them in your work with very young writers and designers:

- Today's writers think about the modes of expression that best communicate their messages in a specific context. I'm thinking about how a preschool teacher invites children to use clay to build a character and then invites them to dress-up and perform in the role of that same character before inviting a bit of reflection on the choices made and how they affected both the creator and the audience. Who preferred to work with clay, and why? Who preferred to perform? Which modes helped each child best bring their character to life?
- They also consider the intended and unintended consequences of their choices, and how they might affect others. As these same children share their clay characters and performances with others, elementary teachers might help them wonder: Which forms seemed to be most appreciated by audience members? Which brought each character to life the best, according to these audiences? How?
- Today's writers purposefully select and combine modes. In this scenario, that might look like inviting young writers to add spatial,

gestural, aural, visual, alphabetic, or haptic features to the characters they've already created. It could look like combining modes to create something entirely new, as well. It's not enough to simply invite this kind of creativity, though. Identifying the choices made and naming their intentions is an important part of explicitly teaching multimodal composition. We might ask: How does this color make your work better? Which words might help us understand this more? What sounds would we hear here? How could you make, record, and embed them? Why would you do that? The answers offered will likely be very self-centered at first. "I made it yellow because I like yellow," is a common sort of response. "I added this picture of my mommy because I love her," you might learn. And this is just fine. Think about how you might follow these responses. What can you model, ask, or invite to deepen their thinking, sharpen their emerging awareness of purpose, and move them toward multimodal composition?

- They choose credible sources and create assets that elevate their compositions. While some might assume that this is the work of upper elementary, middle, and high school writers, even our youngest and least experienced learners are already making meaningful choices here. I'm thinking about how I watched a four-year-old scan the room as everyone was working with finger paint a few months' back. It was his first experience with it, and he began by studying how others were using it. Once he identified an expert painter, he walked over to her table and watched her for a while. Then, he returned to his spot and began replicating her moves. When he was done, he pulled a marker from the tub at the center of the table and added a few illustrations—uninvited.

- They produce work that serves audiences well by informing, moving, and inspiring them to take positive action in service to themselves or others. I'm thinking of the week I spent in the company of young writers who made puppet shows inside of my writing studio. Most of them communicated a powerful theme, and while they took care to create characters and settings that delighted us, it was the positive messaging that really warmed my teacher heart. Do you ever notice how much more attuned some children are to what is right, what is wrong, what is kind, and what is hurtful? When we leverage this sensitivity, even very young writers compose powerful pieces.

Workshop Is Everlasting

Some feel that the writing workshop we've known and loved has failed to serve writers well in these and other endeavors and so, it must be undone. This isn't a perspective that I share. It's my opinion that writing workshops existed long before we schoolified them in any way. They aren't teacher-made constructs, they don't exist to improve test performance of any kind, and they don't need our permission to exist.

When humans come together to create compositions that influence others, workshop happens. I've learned much by simply creating that space and watching what writers do when they find one another there. Decentering myself in this way isn't always easy, but it typically leads to the construction of a workshop that is far more reflective of the writers and designers in the room. They tend to want to create things that are far bigger than print —if I make space for this. Workshop isn't time-boundaried, either. It's everlasting, and what happens within it evolves just as people and places do.

These are the thoughts that I wanted to leave you with before we begin digging into specific and far more practical ideas. When I remember that my experiences, perspectives, and expertise are as narrow as they are expansive, I'm better able to maintain a humble posture as a teacher. I take care to listen and learn from the writers I serve, so that the workshop we create together is one that reflects and serves them well. It's important to align to best practices, but we need to study them at work inside of the workshops we create. When those practices become rules that we no longer reflect upon, we fail to evolve in just-right ways at just-right times. The best writing teachers are agile, reflective, and responsive. They discriminate, and they also take risks.

This is a short book written inside of a short moment in time. It is a microcosm of the mighty writing workshop and one that intends to infuse it with a bit more color, sound, gesture, texture, and vibration. I hope it accomplishes this in ways that those who came before me and those who may follow may never intend. I hope it honors and further amplifies the voices of those who have long reminded us that writing is bigger than print and that young writers are best served by teachers who know that a composition is far more than a collection of written letters and words. I hope it offers practical ideas, approaches, and tools that help you make your writing workshop a space where multimodal composition serves writers and their audiences well.

Let's begin by situating the explicit instruction of multimodal composition inside of the writing workshop we know and love.

Sixty Second Reflection

As you make your way through this book, you'll notice that each chapter ends with a quick invitation to reflect on the content you've just consumed and how you're beginning to contextualize it. I hope these questions inspire meaningful decision-making one chapter at a time. For instance:

- If one were to have asked you what writing was before you read the beginning of the book, how might you have defined it?
- How would you have described a writing workshop?
- How is your thinking, learning, or work beginning to change now?
- What's making you uncomfortable?

References

Arola, K. L., Sheppard, J., & Ball, C. E. (2018). *Writer/designer: A guide to making multimodal projects.* Langara College.

Nicotra, J. (2019). *Becoming rhetorical: analyzing and composing in a multimedia world.* Massachusetts: Cengage.

Shipka, J. (2011). *Toward a composition made whole* (Ser. Pittsburgh series in composition, literacy, and culture). University of Pittsburgh Press.

The New London Group. (1996). A pedagogy of multiliteracies: Designing social futures. *Harvard Educational Review, 66*(1), 60–93.

2
The Multimodal Writing Workshop

When I founded the WNY Young Writers' Studio in Buffalo, New York, in 2008, I had little idea how dramatically my action research within and beyond this community would transform my teaching practice, connect me to a wide professional learning network of others who embrace multimodal composition, and position me as a life-long learner whose best teachers are her students. This is a place where K–12 writers and teachers come together to investigate what constitutes great writing and how to best nurture the writers who might produce it.

During the first handful of years that we met—from 2008 until 2013—I gathered data on 900 writers. Since then, I've had the opportunity to study writers at work in many more workshops, schools, and studios.

It's thanks to the affordances of technology and multimodality that I'm able to invite readers from all over the world into my little Studio today. I refer to my teaching home as Make Writing Studios. I'm grateful to my colleagues and leaders at Daemen College in Amherst, New York, for supporting our learning so well.

Let's wander inside.

I'll introduce you to some of the writers and teachers who workshop there. Try to capture what you see and hear. Consider how this workshop is much like your own and others that have stood the test of time.

A Peek into a Make Writing Studio

We're gathered around a massive table, waiting on the writers. They'll arrive in a little under an hour, and before I shift into writing teacher mode, I want to make sure that I leave the teachers at this table well poised to study whatever it is they've come to study. I can't predict what that might be specifically, I can only create the conditions for it to happen. One wants to learn more about how I teach a mini-lesson that targets multimodal design elements. Another wonders how I confer with young writers and designers. One is interested in pedagogical documentation. Another is eager to see how loose parts are used to make writing. There will be opportunities to study each of these things over the course of the next three hours. We work through the lesson study protocol that will ensure our time is productive, and then, we turn our attention to the materials behind me.

Three long tables feature tubs, trays, and buckets that are overflowing with different loose parts. There are natural elements: shells, pine cones, acorns, and pebbles. There are a few things from my own recycling bin at home: soda caps, scrap cardboard, paper towel tubes, and mail inserts. There are manufactured materials too: LEGO, Play-Doh, Magna-Tiles, buttons, and scrapbooking notions. I share the fire starter that I intend to offer the children, when they enter the room: *When did you last laugh? Use any of these materials to make that memory.* Teachers wonder aloud whether the writers we're about to meet will choose materials they are familiar with or those that are brand new to them. I'm uncertain, and I plan to document what happens. I show them how I plan to use my phone and a small sketchbook to capture what matters here.

Then, it's time to welcome everyone in. They settle into their seats, I share a prompt that invites a bit of making and writing, and they rush to the tables to choose their materials. Most choose the Play-Doh. Some choose markers and small bits of paper. Just a few grab what I imagine might be the most unfamiliar material in the room: the articulated mannequins I purchased on a whim the week prior.

The children are quiet as they create, but tiny smiles tickle the corners of many mouths. I wander the room, peering over shoulders, taking photos, and inviting each of them to tell me more about what they're making. I want to know about the materials they've chosen and why they chose them. Most of these children aren't used to such questions. They shrug, but I can tell that some are thinking about this. Domonique holds up a white feather and offers this right away: "It's soft, like the tree in my yard," she tells me. "The one that dumped a bunch of snow right on top of my little brother after the storm. It was so funny!" Later, she would add these words to her written draft: *The snow looked feathery soft, but it sure wasn't.*

After a few minutes of making, we circle up around the big bulletin board I've positioned in one corner of the room. There are images of other writers and designers there. Some are their ages, others are older. Everyone is a member of our Studio. I want these new members of our community—teachers and young writers alike—to see what's possible. This documentation panel that I've fashioned together shows them what it can look like to make writing in our space. "You'll add new possibilities to this board today," I smile at the small faces peering up at me. "You're already using materials in ways I didn't expect. You're already teaching me so much." And there, I've made another intention clear: They were teachers in this community, as much as I was.

They were also ready to learn a bit more.

Today, we're studying how small body movements reveal a character's feelings. My mini-lesson builds writers' knowledge of these concepts, and we study them inside one of my favorite Pixar animated shorts: *Lifted* (2006). Then, I take care to share several other less familiar mentor texts with them, including a piece of a ballet performance and then a music composition. As I play this last piece for the first time, the teachers in my company look momentarily confused. This passes quickly as hands begin to raise across the room. "I know!" shouts one writer who is completely incapable of containing his glee. "I know where the small body movement could be happening inside the song!" I play it again, and he proceeds to point out a quick series of very light, rapid, high notes that sound different from the rest of the work. "That sounds like a smile," he says. "The rest of the song is kind of sad."

We explore that sweet little simile for a stretch, as well as the way that materials and modes of expression other than written words can actually help us do what those words on paper say, and sometimes, even better.

"So, let's try to do that," I suggest. "When you return to your builds, use loose parts to show us how your character feels. Change what you've made. Make it better."

Mason, one of the writers who offered only a shrug when I asked him why he chose the materials he chose earlier, approaches me as others scurry back to their seats. "Can I use totally different stuff now?" he asks timidly. "Like, different parts?" I tell him that of course, this is fine. "I want to use buttons. I want my character to have big eyes and a big, huge, laughing mouth. Buttons are round, and that works better than the blocks I have now."

"It does," I tell him. I understand his intentions.

As writers tinker, mess, and play, I open my camera and document everything I'm able to. I make some notes about what I see and hear. I'm not sure what it means just yet, and I know that once I have a moment to reflect on all that I've captured, it might mean something different later.

We pause for a snack, and as I send writers off with apples and popcorn, I ask them to think about what's made them proud of themselves so far today. Some of them start chatting about this with one another. Later, we'll draw our answers in our designer's notebooks. We'll circle around the documentation panel again, and we'll add these discoveries to the board.

As snack ends and writers turn back toward their projects, I invite them to transcribe the small part of their stories that they've been making with materials. We've done this each day this week, so they no longer need my modeling or support in order to begin. Some start by labeling every dimension of their builds. These labels will become phrases, sentences, and even whole passages. Others open the Otter.ai app we've been using. They speak their stories into it, and it transcribes what they're saying into written words. Others are telling their stories to partners who listen carefully and then scribble what they've heard onto scraps of paper that they give back to the writer.

I wander from one writer to the next, taking care to document what I'm noticing about how they use the materials and tools offered as well as their mastery of that day's learning targets. I jot notes, snap photos, and ask writers to tell me about the design choices they're making. I audio record their responses over images of their work.

All of us are learning so much.

Later, students will reflect again on where they felt proud of themselves today, which parts of their work were most difficult, and when they felt good about their learning and work. They'll share these reflections with other writers in the room. They'll review some of the photos, videos, and discoveries I'm making. They'll tell me things that these data don't reveal. This will matter.

Tonight or perhaps tomorrow morning, I'll do a bit of after-planning over coffee. Rather than committing hours to the composition of lesson plans ahead of our studio session, I took some time to define the critical concepts we would explore, the mentor texts we would examine, and the learning targets and intentions I was setting for our work together instead. I prepared for my documentation work as well. Now that I've taught the lesson, I am better prepared to write it all down and embed it with links to the images, recordings, and artifacts I'd gathered. I'd share these plans with my wider learning network online. I'd make them available to Studio teachers, too. Some will be grateful for my generosity, but the best of my connections will take some time to reflect with me again. They'll add their perspectives. They'll ask questions. They'll challenge me.

Familiar Territory

While every workshop is reflective of the unique writers in the room and every space they meet in is unique, so much of what you see inside of my Studio is likely quite familiar to you. There are specific features that make a writing workshop a writing workshop, and unless such load-bearing walls are put in place and protected, this construct ceases to exist. These are the essential workshop elements that stand the test of time.

Essential Workshop Elements that Stand the Test of Time

Writing workshop is a place where even our least experienced writers create with intention, for audiences whom they hope to move with their work. Writing isn't produced for the teacher or a grade. It's produced for effect: To make people feel or think or act. It's also a place where young writers and designers explore great writing, tinker around with varied ways to make it, and share their successes and struggles with their peers in order to gain traction and move forward.

Independence is the goal, and interdependence is critical to its achievement. Writing workshop is a place where writers work in partnership with others—including the teacher—throughout the entire process. They pay attention to the different moves that writers make. They consider their intended consequences and the unintended and sometimes surprising results that follow. This is how they learn that composition is messy stuff, that growth happens through struggle and revision, and that every writer develops their own approaches as they learn more from their false starts. Sharing our learning is an important part of this work. Often, teacher-directed mini-lessons consume far less time than writer and designer-led demonstrations. Even when writers are very young and very inexperienced.

I remember when Jacey made her first story in my Studio. Somebody wanted something in her story, but of course there was a problem. Specifically, her mommy wanted chocolate chip cookies, but when she went to the cupboard, she discovered that someone had eaten her secret stash! The somebody/wanted/but/so frame may be a one that you're familiar with (Macon, Bewell, & Vogt, 1994).

Jacey was, too. And even though she was just four years old, she used fresh tubs of yellow and red and brown Play-Doh to build those first three story elements, and then, she spoke about them with me. I audio recorded her story one panel at a time, and then, I handed her my phone so she could listen to her story, over and over again. I shifted my attention to the next writer in the room, but this didn't deter Jacey. I noticed her in my peripheral vision, grabbing a pencil, and stringing emergent letters together across a page of primary paper. As a young teacher, I never attempted these approaches, and I wonder now how this might have elevated the workshop I once knew.

So, What Makes a Multimodal Writing Workshop Different?

Everything that I've learned about writing workshops that support multimodal composition I've learned from the composers themselves. Nearly every moment I've spent in their company has been fairly well documented, and coding these data revealed the following distinctions to me. It's important that I mention this because your findings may vary, and when they do, I hope to hear from you. We are all learners here—I just happened to write books about what I'm noticing. I'm not an expert, and I have no desire to be a guru. If you're in this work, I'm your colleague, and I'd love to learn from you.

One of the greatest things I've discovered: Play is not a developmental phase that we should be ushering young writers through. It's an essential element of high quality workshops for writers of all ages and experience levels. Loose parts play, in particular, provides writers with materials that may be used symbolically, metaphorically, and most importantly—rapidly—in order to generate and communicate complex ideas that we may not yet have enough print power to pull off with written words. So while many of you may teach inside of workshops that invite building, drawing, and even moments of inventive play, I worry that we make these fleeting experiences that are intended to merely engage young writers, finesse those who are frustrated, and serve as scaffolds for others who are striving to put down proficient print. Play is not our plaything, and yet, too often, it's treated this way. Play is serious stuff, and when it's absent from our writing workshops, it undermines the work that happens there.

Here's something else: In a multimodal writing workshop, the mentor texts we value and investigate are not made with written words alone. Design lives beside writer's craft as we pursue inquiry work together and offer moments of explicit instruction. Rather than following prefabricated lesson plans, unit plans, and templates, teachers invite writers to investigate the forms they wish to experiment and tinker with. They begin to notice what they share in common in terms of writing as well as design, and they pursue writing processes that are distinctly multimodal. Sometimes, teacher-led mini-lessons are used to deepen this learning, but just as often, writers work independently or in partnership with other writers through these investigations and the teacher remains decentered in the process. Standards, learning targets, and teaching points are essential to this work, but a far more agile and responsive process is used to define, prioritize, and align them within and across grade levels and even content areas. I'll discuss this more in Chapters 4 and 5.

Teachers typically position themselves a bit differently inside of multimodal writing workshops as well. They still ask pointed questions that allow them to offer meaningful and criteria-specific feedback. They also invite writers to use a rich variety of promising strategies. These strategies attend to the purpose and craft of writing as well as the application of design choices that are specific to the modes and media that writers are experimenting with. They're also sensitive to each writer's unique history, talents, experiences, and identity. As it's nearly impossible for any teacher or writer within such a workshop to fully understand what such sensitivity requires, agreements are established within the workshop that normalize boundary setting, the seeking of agency, and conflict resolution. Teachers commit to humble practice, assuming that they don't know what they don't know, and regarding the children they serve as their primary and most important teachers. Andrea Schaber, a kindergarten teacher in Chappaqua Central School District in New York State serves as a role model for me and for many other teachers who know her. Read in the appendix more about her experiences with multimodal composition, what her students have taught her, and how she's evolving as a workshop teacher. She is one who consistently commits to humble practice.

The role of documentation cannot be underestimated here, and this is perhaps what distinguishes a multimodal writing workshop like the one I'm describing from those I was trained to create as a pre-service and then as a young and inexperienced teacher.

According to John Hattie, whose meta-research was published in the highly acclaimed book *Visible Learning* (2009), when teachers see learning through the eyes of students and invite those students to become their own teachers, growth is exponential (Hattie, 2009, pp. 25–26). Documenting learning made visible by writers and teachers alike is an essential component of the multimodal writing workshops I build and strive to sustain.

To accomplish this, my relationship with writers and the workshop they create must be respectful, reciprocal, and responsive. Experience has taught me that my passion for this work benefits many, but I'm wise enough to know that I need to manage this passion well. It can prevent me from noticing things I need to. Where passion feeds my biases, documentation humbles me. It unravels my expectations and challenges my assumptions. It reminds me that writers and their workshops existed long before any expert invited them into any school. They are owned by no one, and for me to be of any service at all, they must be seen. They must be heard. And I must be willing to be uncertain and even wrong. Often.

Documentation invites all of us—teachers and writers alike—to capture what we see and hear, reflect alone and then together, and pose theories that are grounded in those lived workshop experiences. This doesn't mean that we ignore our expertise. It does provide consistent and powerful opportunities to interrogate it, though.

Four Ways to Situate Multimodal Composition Inside of Your Current Writing Workshop

Making space for multimodal composition doesn't have to be an overwhelming endeavor. In fact, most elementary teachers that I know feel that they are offering at least some opportunity for this throughout each workshop year. It's how they position multimodal expression within the process that makes the most difference. Too often, elementary teachers are pressured to push through moments of making as quickly as possible, to push writers toward their "real" work—producing print. When writers begin drawing their stories in kindergarten, this excites us. When they still prefer to draw in third grade, we begin to wring our hands a bit. Like many, I once worried that dedicating time to composing multimodally would compromise writers' ability to use written words. When I finally began making space for multimodal composition, I worried that writers wouldn't be able to finish the complex projects they were pursuing and that my limited experience and understanding of certain modes, their affordances, and the tools that enabled writers to work with them would result in fast, collective failure. And this was true, sometimes.

Each of these experiences offered important lessons, and I want to share them with you. Hopefully, my struggles will benefit your beginning and offer good company for the road ahead. Here's how you might begin to reimagine your workshop and make space for multimodal composition.

Begin with Identity Work

Is the All About Me project still taking up significant space at the start of your new school year? I love these invitations for very young writers to share more about who they are. I'm wondering how we might make the average All About Me project a bit more meaningful, though. What questions might we ask, and what could we learn about where young writers are really coming from, how their history has shaped them, and how we might serve them better, in light of their more complex identities?

This is crucial work, if we're to create spaces where all writers truly shape the workshop. Defining concepts that are critical to identity such as religion, race, gender, and ability offers young writers more than a vocabulary but lenses to read and write and connect with others through. Exploring the identity of different characters inside of the multimodal mentor texts we study, challenging common stereotypes, and inviting the young writers we serve to self-identify in ways that help everyone know one another better and more importantly—respect each other even more—fosters a truly creative culture. Multimodal composition is culturally rooted. Most of your students speak and write these languages, regardless of their experience with print. Identity work helps us understand where we come from individually and what might create collectively when our whole selves are welcome in our workshops.

A Peek Inside a Make Writing Studio Session

Once I began to better understand the influence of identity on the cultures we were creating inside of my own workshop, the invitations I typically extended to primary and elementary writers at the start of each year no longer seemed quite as meaningful. Still, I really wrestled with the unintended consequences of asking very young children to think about things like race, gender, ability, and religion and how these things deeply shape who we are and how we are in the world. I doubted that the youngest writers I served would even understand these words. I worried that speaking openly about identity would illuminate difference and create distance.

And I was wrong.

Quite a few of the students in my Studio—and in the school districts I visited, too—not only understood these concepts, but they were excited to discuss them. They were proud of their identities, and they were delighted to meet story characters and classmates who shared things in common with them. They also demonstrated tremendous empathy when we discussed things like stereotyping and the other ways we might hurt people's feelings if we don't take care to understand their identities better.

Now, my work with primary and elementary writers typically begins by inviting them to reflect on questions like those you see in Figure 2.1. They shape individual responses, and we talk about them together. They meet others in the room who share their identities, and they learn more about how to welcome, appreciate, and learn from those who are different from them.

EXPLORING OUR IDENTITIES
What about us makes us who we are?

Race
How do I like to describe the color of my skin?

How do I like to describe the texture of my hair?

What words do I use to describe my race?

Ability
What does my body do well?

What does my brain do well?

What are my talents?

What does my body or brain have a hard time doing?

Ethnicity
What languages do I speak?

Which beliefs are most important to my family?

Which foods do we eat when we celebrate holidays?

Gender
Do I describe myself as a boy?

Do I describe myself as a girl?

Neither?

Both?

Figure 2.1 Exploring Our Identities

If you're seeking other meaningful ways to approach this work, you'll find additional instructional resources in the appendix, with more material available at https://angelastockman.com/resources-2/.

One simple way to begin involves creating an expertise chart for your workshop. Here, writers reveal their unique strengths and interests, so that others may turn to them for unique kinds of support. Consider beginning each workshop week by asking writers to name who they intend to learn from. Consider ending each week by inviting them to share their experiences and a bit of gratitude, too.

Grow Your Curricular Toolkit

Experienced writing workshop teachers maintain a toolkit of learning targets, teaching points, and strategies that help writers develop valuable skills. They curate mentor texts and connect with those who have created them online or through other professional learning opportunities. They collect lessons and units and curriculum resources as well. Those who are inexperienced might rely on pre-fabricated programs heavily. As experience is gained, seasoned workshop teachers often become excited to design their own. Embrace this opportunity to widen and deepen your perspective of what writing is and how it is best taught. It's okay to plan, but many find that their best lessons are those their students led them to, quite unexpectedly.

"But how do I know what lessons to teach?" I'm often asked. "Which learning targets should I attend to? And where do I find multimodal mentor texts?" These are fair questions, and I've left helpful tools for you in the appendix. Have a peek at the last page of the Feedback Structures, Protocols, and Frames for Writers and Designers.

While it might be more efficient for me to simply hand you explicit teaching points, learning targets, or intentions, experience has taught me that this does more harm than good. It's important for you to design these anchors in response to your students' very unique interests and needs. It's important to know how to find just-right mentor texts and help learners use them as tools. Writers' purposes are varied; the six modes of expression combine in countless ways to achieve varied effects, and the media, platforms, and tools that writers use to create and share their compositions are ever-changing. If you simply lift and drop my constructs, you'll fail to serve your students well.

I know that's daunting. All of these unpredictabilities were probably hardest for me to accept as I transitioned from teaching the production of written words to serving multimodal composers. I know that predictability, alignment, and even constraint serve writers well. It took some time for me to learn how to design curriculum that was aligned yet agile and that controlled for creativity as well as it controlled for quality. I'll speak more about curriculum design in Chapter 6. For now, consider these shifts:

1. **Make space for writers to explore and then compose for varied purposes.** They might begin the year assuming a storytelling stance, producing shadow puppet shows or video recording stop-motion videos. Then, a second unit or writing experience might inspire them to assume a teaching stance, conducting research individually or collaboratively to produce infographics. They might share their opinions by creating Flipgrid campaigns, and they might use that content to identify opinions that are worth making an evidence-based argument about.
2. **Plan to explore familiar alphabetic or print-centric texts that were created for similar purposes, and work together to define their elements**. For example, even if writers intend to create multimodal stories, you might begin by exploring a variety of narratives that are primarily composed of written words and illustrations first, in order to define their common features. Acquiring knowledge of these fundamental concepts is a critical first step, and doing so within the context of a form that is familiar to writers is clarifying (Stern et al., 2021, p. 18).
3. **Next, analyze a variety of multimodal texts that were designed to achieve similar purposes.** You might explore how characters are introduced in a children's book as compared to a puppet show or an animated short. You might explore how opinions are in an advertisement, on a billboard, and in a commercial. Notice what these very different kinds of compositions have in common with those that were created with written words alone. Notice how each piece is different. Analyze the design choices made by each creator. Consider the affordances of each mode of expression. What does one offer that others cannot? Analyze how the creator leveraged just-right tools in order to design and share each work.
4. **Define and invite writers to create within clear structures.** Figure 2.2, which is also included in my book *Creating Inclusive Writing Environments in the K–12 Classroom: Reluctance, Resistance, and Strategies*

that Make a Difference (2021), reflects how any multimodal informational text might be organized. Whether the text is made with written words or a combination of other modes, many informational texts will include these elements. If writers know the structure, they can use the modes they're most comfortable with to compose. I've left additional structures in the Planning Tools available for download here: https://angelastockman.com/resources-2/. These are perspectives, not prescriptions, but you might appreciate them.

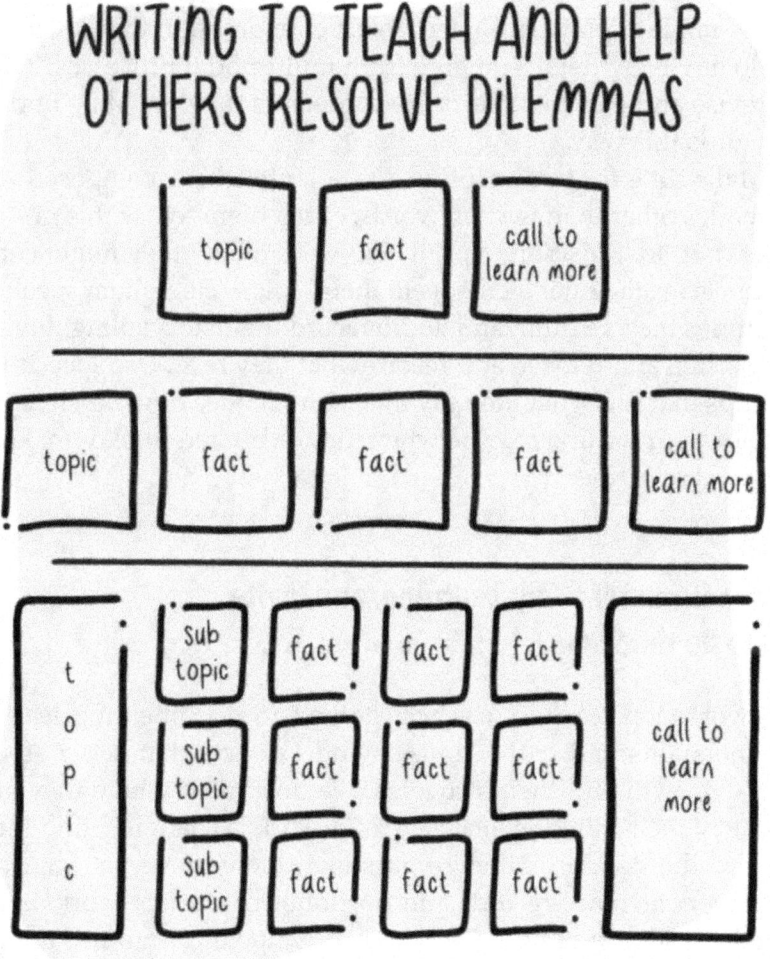

Figure 2.2 Writing to Teach and Help Others Resolve Dilemmas

5. **Invite a multimodal creative process in service to written words.** For instance, if a writer knows that the story they plan to create includes a character who expects one thing to happen, is surprised when an entirely different thing happens, and is changed for the better as a result, they might define the structure of their story in this way: Beginning/Character + Middle/Surprise + Ending/ Positive Change. They might build this plan with LEGOs or mold it with clay. They might draw it. They might tell it to a friend or use an app to audio record it. They might choose to perform it, instead. This feels and functions a bit like the rehearsal phase of writing that so many of us writing workshop teachers are familiar with, but it's a bit different. Each material and mode of expression that writers call into play empowers a sort of expression that other modes do not. New details emerge from multimodal processes. They revise and elevate their original ideas as they go. They find better words this way.
6. **Make time for transcription.** Once writers have composed with modes other than written words, coach them to use this prototype or draft to transition to print. Show them how they might construct labels for the finer elements in their builds. Help them speak the stories they've built, and audio record their storytelling. Invite them to listen and relisten and record what they hear. Use speech-to-text apps that flip what they say into print. Notice how much more complex their writing may be when they're invited to play, make, and then transcribe.

Prepare to Document Your Learning, and Invite Writers to Do the Same

Writing workshop teachers are accustomed to documenting learning. We make annotations and gather images and artifacts that serve as evidence of writers' growth and their struggles. We document where they are in the process; how their thinking, learning, and work is changing; and their progress toward the standards they're pursuing. Many of us are accustomed to maintaining conference records and portfolios of student work. Some of us dedicate consistent time to reflection, and we take care to use the evidence gleaned from this practice to inform our own. Do most writing teachers document their own learning? Do they invite writers to do the same? Or are our documentation practices strictly aligned to our pre-planned units, lessons, rubrics, and scoring criteria?

Documentation is about discovery, and there is no better time to engage in a documentation project of your own than now, as you begin to try something wholly unfamiliar to you. A documentation project begins with the definition of a concept that you'd like to study. Choose one that matters to you and that matters to your students. I focused my first documentation project on resistance in the writing workshop. Then, I spent a year documenting everything I noticed in relation to that concept. I took photos, recorded interviews with writers during conferences, captured video, and curated work samples and process work. I encourage you to do the same, in service to your greater learning. I encourage you to adopt documentation as a daily discipline, too. Document what you notice about writers' progress toward each day's learning target. Use what you discover to inform your next steps. You'll know that you're making real progress as a documentarian if your findings serve to challenge your assumptions and reveal your biases to you. This is what makes this work so valuable. In the absence of it, I find myself becoming far more certain than I deserve to be. That's problematic in a thousand different ways.

If you're interested in exploring a variety of documentation projects in process and beginning one of your own, you might appreciate the Studying Learning document available for download here: https://angelastockman.com/resources-2/. It includes tools that will help you document daily progress toward teaching points. Don't hesitate to reach out to me on social media if you'd like to collaborate more and in the company of similarly spirited workshop teachers. I'd love to get to know you and welcome you into that fold, and to share my current documentation project with you.

Confer with Careful Intention

Conferring is the heart of the workshop. This is the place where we learn how to actively listen and genuinely speak with writers in a way that lifts their spirits as well as the quality of their work. These exchanges are not intended to evaluate and remediate writers but instead, grow in relationship with them. This is how writers learn to serve one another—by experiencing the service we offer them.

Multimodal composition has elevated the writing workshops that I facilitate in many ways, but its effect on my relationships with writers has been most profound. When I privileged print inside of my writing workshops, I know that I alienated many young writers whose compositional strengths lay within modes of expression that I made no room for and regarded far too little. This arrogance prevented me from knowing my students completely, and I've since realized this was not only their loss, but mine as well. When writers are invited to express themselves using every mode of expression and tool at their disposal, they call upon those they're most experienced and comfortable with. Their hidden talents are brought into sharp relief, and this inspires and empowers others.

I cannot tell you how I have grown as a teacher and a writer because of this. I cannot tell you how this shift will add texture and complexity to your workshop. I cannot tell you how important multimodal composition is to the creation of truly inclusive writing communities. This is something that you and your students need to experience for yourselves. It is something that cannot and should not ever be denied.

In my last book, *Creating Inclusive Writing Environments in the K–12 Classroom: Reluctance, Resistance, and Strategies that Make a Difference* (2021), I devote a significant amount of time to the exploration of cultural archetypes. The distinction between communal and individualistic cultures is well documented, and the implications for our work as writing teachers are profound. When we define writing as the production of written words alone, we do more harm than we might imagine. Writing is far more than that, it always has been, and the fact that we haven't attended to this reality says much about our cultural and racial history. Schools were built by individualists for individualists. Writing workshop was as well. Multimodal composition recognizes and celebrates diversity in expression, and this is essential to the creation of equitable, anti-racist writing workshops.

If conferring is the heart of the writing workshop, then what we say and how we say it matters very much. This isn't new thinking. Experienced writing teachers have always been attuned to this reality. What's different is that workshops that invite multimodal composition recognize the importance of print, but they don't necessarily privilege it.

Writers aren't characterized as struggling if they fail to produce written words and instead, choose to build or draw or perform their texts instead. Our goal isn't to help them transition multimodal process work to alphabetic text or print, either. Our goal is to serve writers through a decision making process that challenges them to choose the best modes of expression for their intended messages and audiences. This is challenging work, and it calls us to frame our feedback with careful intention.

These are the steps that I take when I'm approaching a writer and their work with the intention to be of service to them:

- **Ask.** I ask them what they are creating, and I listen and often document their response.
- **Look and Listen.** I consider the unique goal that the writer might be working toward that day. It might have shown up in a mini-lesson or in the learning target that the whole class is focused on. It might relate to the element of the structure or form that the writer is experimenting with. It might be the result of solution-finding, tinkering, or play. I look for evidence of the writer's progress toward that goal—that thing that the writer is trying to do—using whatever modes of expression they've chosen. I also look for evidence of struggle and areas of investment that I hadn't anticipated or invited the writer to commit to.
- **Offer.** I *offer* criteria-specific warm feedback that speaks to what the writer is doing well, what is present in their work, or what they're showing me they're ready to try, given the progress they've made. I *offer* a strategy that intends to move them forward, and I typically share my own example or more importantly, those *offered* by other writers in the room. If it's possible to offer a variety of approaches without overwhelming the writer, I take care to do this. Too often, strategies are received as directives instead of options. *Offering* a few prevents this from happening.
- **Ask Again.** Then, I ask the writer to tell me how they might make use of what we've explored together. Here, I usually learn whether my feedback was helpful or not. If necessary, I reframe it and try again. Sometimes, this isn't necessary, though. Sometimes, writers reject my ideas because chatting with me helps them find their own way forward.

As a writer and a writing teacher, I maintain a profound love for the written word. As a result, the feedback frames, strategies, and examples that I'm accustomed to sharing tend to privilege print. Learning how to speak the language of multimodal composition has been important learning and work. How might you use the tool you see in Figure 2.3 to find new words yourself?

SPEAKING THE LANGUAGE OF MULTIMODAL COMPOSITION

These six concepts can be found at play inside of many multimodal compositions. I'm grateful to Kristin L. Arola, Jennifer Sheppard, and Cheryl E. Ball for pushing my thinking about what constitutes craft so that I might frame more meaningful feedback.

Emphasis

Which details are most important?

How might you design them in a way that makes them stand out?

Which details are less important? How might you make them less noticeable?

Contrast

Which parts are very different from one another?

How might you demonstrate this?

Which parts are similar? How can you illustrate this?

Organization

How should the parts fit together?

How might you design them in a way that makes sense?

What would happen if you changed the order? How might you tinker with that?

Color

What mood or message are you trying to create?

How might you use color to do this?

What if you removed most--or all-- of the color from this work?

Proximity

How does closeness and distance matter in your work?

How might you design this piece in a way that communicates this?

What happens when you play with proximity?

Alignment

How do the elements of your piece relate to one another?

How could you show us this in your work?

Is messiness meaningful in your work? How will you use it?

Figure 2.3 Speaking the Language of Multimodal Composition

Sixty Second Reflection

Before you turn the final page of this chapter, take a moment to summarize and reflect upon what you've learned.

- What are the essential elements of every writing workshop?
- How do they present themselves differently inside of workshops where multimodal composition occurs?

- What's resonating with you?
- Where are you sensing your own resistance?
- What will you need to investigate further in order to situate multimodal composition inside of your writing workshop with meaningful intention?
- How is your thinking, learning, or work beginning to change?

References

Arola, K. L., Sheppard, J., & Ball, C. E. (2018). *Writer/designer: A guide to making multimodal projects.* Langara College.

Hattie, J. (2009). *Visible learning: A synthesis of over 800 meta-analyses relating to achievement.* Routledge.

Macon, J. M., Bewell, D., & Vogt, M. E. (1994). *Responses to literature.* Newark: International Reading Association.

Pixar Animation Studios. (2006). *Lifted.* Retrieved from https://youtu.be/58Na0-C1e2U.

Stern, J. H., Ferraro, K. F., Duncan, K., Aleo, T., Hattie, J., & Zhao, Y. (2021). *Learning that transfers: Designing curriculum for a changing world.* Corwin.

Stockman, A. (2021). *Creating inclusive writing environments in the K–12 classroom: Reluctance, resistance, and strategies that make a difference.* Routledge.

Part 2

How Do We Create Multimodal Writing Workshops?

3

A Blueprint for the Multimodal Writing Workshop

The gymnasium in Good Shepherd School doubled as our cafeteria, and every Wednesday we were invited to buy a hot lunch there. Our hot lunches typically consisted of slices from the only pizzeria in town, lettuce softened in a marinade of thick Italian dressing, and my favorite: cold bottles of Cherry Crush. We pulled them from the coin-operated soda machine that spent the rest of the week keeping the local bingo players hydrated.

The door to the parking lot and playing fields was situated to the left of that machine, and this made for an interesting juxtaposition. Once, I was asked to identify a single childhood setting where my personal heaven and hell collided, and I imagined that far corner of my school cafeteria. Here, my Cherry Crush jubilation was tempered by the knowledge that there was precious little time to savor my treat. We were given minutes to eat and then marched outside to skip rope, run bases, and participate in other physical feats that were nothing like the more civil endeavors that I preferred: reading and writing and drawing on big sheets of butcher paper with scented markers.

So, you might imagine how I felt when one day, instead of bracing myself for another round of dodgeball, I watched my teacher carry a curious collection of materials across the playground and toward the weathered bench at the edge of the baseball diamond. I remember how she waved us over and then invited us to gather up a handful of autumn leaves.

"We'll use blueprint paper to make photos of them with the sun," she explained. But first, she invited us to study how each leaf was composed.

Learning the Language of Leaves

I remember noticing how they felt—the rough certainty of each vein and rib that rose across the smooth leaf plates. Greener leaves were softer than those that had already turned red or yellow or my favorite shade of orange. Before this lesson, leaves were a generality to me, but from that moment forward, I began to see them in vivid, granular detail, and this stuck with me.

How strange it was then, just a short while later, to contemplate those blueprints after our work on the baseball diamond was done. The sun rendered these crisp and colorful creations into ghostly negatives that left so much more to our imaginations. I took all of my blueprints home, cut them out, and glued microscopic bits of tissue paper between the bright white lines that illuminated each leaf's margins. I remember appreciating the prints that my classmates made and how each was similar to mine but also very different.

I wonder now how they roughed their own collections in. What colors did they choose? Which materials? And why?

Each time I begin to imagine a new writing workshop experience, I remember this small moment from my childhood. I try to honor the most important learning that happened inside of it. It's unlikely that my teacher intended to inspire my life-long interest in the relationship between constraint, creativity, and identity, but this was the unintended consequence of her literacy-rich science lesson, and in many ways, this entire chapter is, too.

Before you go any further here, close your eyes and imagine your ideal writing workshop. Perhaps it's the one where you currently teach. Think about the way you build relationships there and the way you work to gain the trust of the young writers you serve. Consider how you deepen each participant's self-awareness and all that you do to create a welcoming and inspiring learning environment for them. How do you plan to teach? What does instruction look like? What materials are offered, and which routines and rituals are essential to all of you?

Write or doodle or draw your responses to these questions. Then, gather the pages you fill much like leaves in your own hands. Set them on a mat of metaphorical blueprint paper in the sun, and notice the negative that emerges.

You've exposed something important here: the essential elements of your writing workshop. If you were to remove any one of those veins, mid-ribs, leaf-plates, or margins, that workshop would cease to be a workshop. Your blueprint defines its load-bearing walls.

Defining Your Workshop's Load-bearing Walls

Experienced workshop teachers will tell you that the environment they create with writers, the curriculum they create, and their instructional approaches shape-shift in response to what they discover about their students and what they learn about how to improve their practice. There are a few things that are fundamental to any writing workshop. If these things were removed, the workshop would cease to exist.

Workshop is a wonderfully humbling place. Humility is something teachers practice with intention here. Rather than positioning themselves at the front of the room to share their expertise and directives, workshop teachers situate themselves beside writers—in collaboration with them. They situate themselves behind them as well to listen, watch, notice, and learn from them. Inquiry is the heart of all learning in a writer's workshop, and that inquiry is done in service to others. Teachers create in service to young writers. Writers create in service to real audiences. Even our youngest writers and designers workshop products that are shared with people other than their teachers, classmates, families, and friends. Those audiences genuinely appreciate their work as well.

It takes time to learn how to create a community like the one I've just described. This is the work of a lifetime, not a year or a unit or a day. This work is a vocation, a commitment, and a gift. It's also a collaboration between teachers, writers, and the wider communities that each and both are a part of.

It makes sense then that like leaves on a tree, all workshops evolve a bit differently in response to their climate and changes in the weather. Their distinguishing features make them easy to identify wherever we may find them. Have a peek at Figure 3.1. When we study writing workshop blueprints, these are the white lines that expose their load-bearing walls:

- Writing workshops invite learning experiences that deepen self-awareness.
- They're founded on agreements, protocols, and intentions that build trusting relationships.
- Writing workshops employ culturally sustaining curricula, instruction, and assessments.
- They prepare writers to produce multimodal compositions for real audiences beyond their circle of teachers, peers, and family members.

Does that seem murky? It should. Rigid structures serve few people well inside of any workshop, and they're also impossible to sustain. John Lienhard

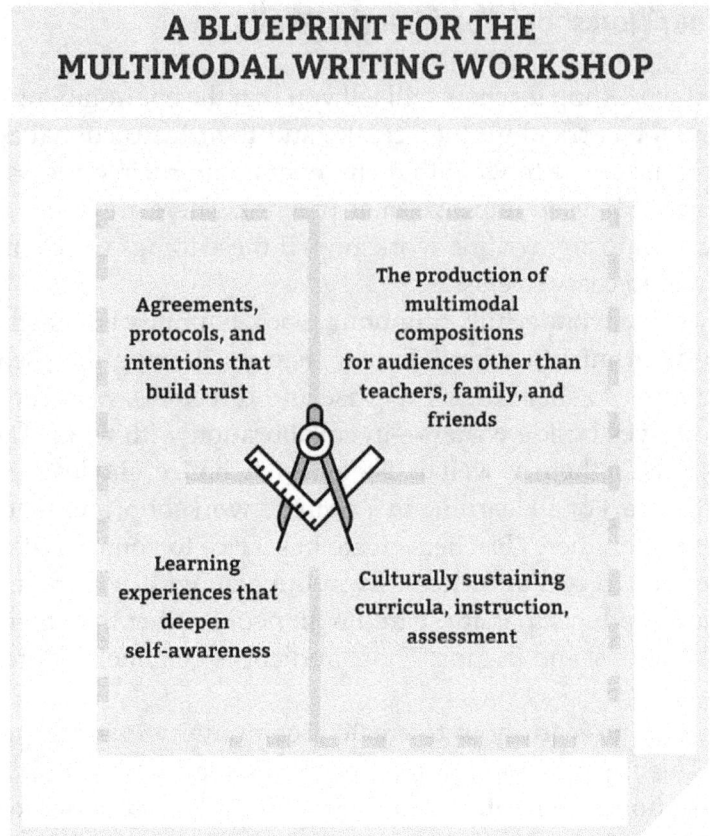

Figure 3.1 A Blueprint for the Multimodal Writing Workshop

(1993), Professor Emeritus of Mechanical Engineering and History at the University of Phoenix, reminds us that blueprints are feathery things. Almost ghostly in their appearance, they require inventors (as all writing workshop teachers are) to see "darkly—as through a glass" (Lienhard, 1993, Episode 802). This is our genius, he reminds us, our willingness to bridge two worlds. While the ethereal blueprint of the workshop we hold in our mind's eye is a gauzy vision of a community, it's brought into sharp relief as young writers and designers rough it in.

This truth underpins nearly every tension I've experienced throughout my career. I teach writing because I know that competent writers are better able to advocate for themselves and others out there in the big, wide world. Writing is freedom. It's liberation from a thousand different forms of oppression, including those we impose upon ourselves. This is why, in my opinion, there are no benign writing teachers. We're either serving this greater good or we're compromising it. It's difficult to believe that fuzzy blueprints prepare any teacher to rise to that occasion, but remembering the metaphor of the leaf has been helpful every time I struggle here.

When my vision of what a workshop is or should be is too sharp, I end up doing more harm than good. Those white lines inside of our blueprints reveal our workshop's supporting structures, and they matter. If we remove them, we render it unrecognizable. And yet, if we rough-in that frame all by ourselves, the workshop becomes a reflection of who we are, what we need, and what we intend to impose on learners. Blueprints are tools that can put us in relationship with them instead. They invite co-creation within a carefully calculated but purposefully incomplete frame. Let's study each component closely and consider different approaches that make this collaborative design process productive and rewarding.

Creating Learning Experiences that Deepen Self-Awareness

Self-awareness refers to our understanding of who we are, where we come from, how our experiences have shaped us, and how others perceive us. Self-aware teachers understand that their personal, cultural, and racial histories influence the way they shape the writing workshops they create and relate to the writers they serve there. They understand implicit bias and take care to design learning experiences that reduce it. They also commit to daily reflective practices and enter into critical friend groups that make the likelihood of uncovering their own biases, learning, and changing much greater. None of this is about shame. All teachers must commit to this work. We all carry biases. We can all support one another without judgment if we recognize this.

As you begin to develop a vision for your future writing workshop, you might find yourself contemplating activities that invite writers to define where they're from, what interests them, and who takes up space in their hearts. These are beautiful invitations. I encourage you to begin by getting to know yourself a bit better first. I speak to this at length in Chapter 4 of *Creating Inclusive Writing Environments in the K–12 Writing Workshop: Reluctance, Resistance, and Strategies that Make a Difference* (2021). There, I share a variety of approaches for gaining and then sustaining greater self-awareness. My intentions in that book were a bit different than those that are motivating this one. I hoped that readers would close that cover with a heightened awareness of the assumptions we've made about writers we label "strugglers." I devoted a substantial amount of that text to the exploration of cultural archetypes, and if I achieved anything, I know it was this: Those who read that text cannot claim that they aren't aware of the effects of white supremacy on writing instruction in American schools. They can't claim uncertainty about how to do better, either. And they certainly can't put me or any other charismatic proponent of writing workshop up on any pedestal that protects us from distinguishing our intentions from our influence. When I speak to strengthening our self-awareness, I speak to the fact that we all have so much learning to do about who writers are, what writing really is, and how it's evolved inside of cultures other than those we come from. Including me.

Practicing self-awareness means that I must remember that I come from predominantly white, central European people. I was raised Catholic, attended Catholic primary and elementary schools, and earned my teaching certification from the State University of New York College at Fredonia, where most of my instructors were brilliant, creative, and incredibly supportive upper middle class white males. They provided my induction into writing workshop, introduced me to the work of Donald Graves and Nancie Atwell, and eventually, ensured that I was able to student teach inside of a rural school system that was invested in that model, which was just beginning to take the field by storm.

No one shared the history of writing workshop as we've come to define it in K–12 school back then, and I didn't go looking for it myself. I trusted the experts and did my best to keep my head above water while student teaching and then, moving into my own classroom. I've learned much over the last 30 years, and all of it has given me great pause.

We all stand on the shoulders of giants, I know. I'm grateful for the contributions of each and every one. I'm also far more aware of where their ideas originated from and even more importantly, why I was and still remain so attracted to them.

I know I need to take good care here, because the writing workshops I create and sustain don't need me to make any choices for them to be inequitable. They are, like so many systems, inherently so. Writing workshop does need me to consciously and consistently seek out and address inequities. Writers need me to actively disrupt them. And so, while it is not my purview to lead equity work, and I have no intention of doing that here or anywhere else, it is my responsibility to ensure that the writing workshops I influence are rooted in soil that fortifies very diverse human beings. It's my responsibility to remind myself—and perhaps you, too—that our identities are everything, that inequity is woven into the fabric of our schools and our writing workshops, and that we must invite and welcome the exploration of that reality. We must hold one another accountable here as well.

There are many ways to accomplish this. I began by reading the work of scholars whose voices have not been heard because they've been historically marginalized. At the same time, I began following many of these same people on social media and seeking out critical friends who were willing to engage with me as I was learning. I began hiring equity readers, and they put critical feedback on the things that I was writing. Their perspective didn't simply tighten my texts—it deepened my self-awareness as well. Finally, I committed to frequent journaling, and I began sharing some of what I was discovering about myself, how I've tended to define writing and identify writers in far more public forums. This was necessary, because it put me in relationship with readers who did not know or necessarily care about me. These were the people who were better able to call me in or out, school me about all that I didn't know, and hold me more accountable for doing better.

This is how you might begin centering multimodal composition inside of your own writing workshop and even, your wider system: Consistently communicate the message that making, performing, tinkering, and playing produce stronger writers and writing. Demonstrate how the playful work we do in the early grades is not some mere bridge to a better land, but rich territory that we'd do well to sustain far beyond elementary school. Writers, teachers, parents, and people in power must come to understand that if we're to build better writers of all ages, we need to make more space for multimodal composition in every workshop at every grade level. Elementary teachers know this. You have evidence of how this works. And yet, many of you still feel yourselves pressured to replace opportunities for multimodal composition with exercises that instead build print power. Drawing is treated as a developmental step in the writing process that writers should move through and then abandon once they've achieved a certain facility with the written word. Play is the stuff of primary school. And the arts become peripheral, as if they're some sort of icing on the content cake. In my experience, when we bring multimodal composition into our writing workshops, we nurture multiple literacies, and the written work that emerges is elevated as well. The notion that it must be brought there at all saddens me. I think it's already there for many of you. If it isn't, I have a feeling that's because you were coerced into putting it away, like so many childish playthings. Exploring your experiences, tapping into your own wisdom, and owning what you know about the influence of multimodality on literacy development is an important way to reclaim some parts of your self-awareness that you've tucked away. I hope this book gives you that permission.

This might inspire you to create or sustain a workshop where writers can show up as their whole selves and where they are able to become increasingly self-aware. I'm uncertain if I ever fully accomplished this. I'm uncertain if I ever will. I know much more about what it looks like to try at this point in my own learning journey. Here's the best of what I know right now: Creating this kind of space challenges us to offer more consistent and intentional invitations. They must be bigger than the All About Me project, the bio-poem, or the "Where I'm from" pieces that I still invite writers to create and share, because they matter. I know from experience how those invitations can ease our entry into deliberate and collective self-awareness work. I have to remember that they're only a beginning. More importantly: This important work requires sensitivity and humility, too.

It's tempting to charge forward with good intentions, speaking and writing from the heart about our vision of an equitable writing workshop, sharing bold and brilliant ideas, and posing meaningful questions that aim to open writers up and meet one another empathetically. Here's something that my own experiences and eventually—mistakes—taught me: Children do not owe us their stories. In fact, some children work very hard to compartmentalize aspects of their identities and repress their stories. You'd be surprised to know how many young writers live this way. Children don't owe us answers about who they are, where they're from, or what their interests and needs are. Inviting them to define and share these things can often feel quite threatening. Children shouldn't have to play along when asked to reveal things about themselves that they don't spend much time thinking about, and they certainly don't owe details and explanations. We owe writers workshops where they can show up as their entire selves without fear of being judged, shamed, or even recognized as special simply because they're different. That's all well and good in theory, but how do we create safer spaces? How do we create workshops where children can reveal only what they choose about their identities but still enjoy absolute confidence that what they experience will reveal and attend to their interests and needs?

I'm finding that this is less about adding new lessons, tools, or interventions and more about stepping back, loosening up, and making more space for different kinds of writers to do different kinds of things in our community.

For instance, I'm beginning to make much more space for writers to use the languages they truly speak. There is no such thing as a superior language, after all. Languages are developed by the communities they serve. They shift to sustain their utility, they spread between cultural groups as speakers move within and beyond their own communities, and they die when they're no longer useful (Holmes & Wilson, 2017). The myth of superior languages was dispelled long ago, and the assumption that the languages of low-income groups and those that live in specific settings are less complex or rule-governed is a bit of ignorance that privilege and racism perpetuate. I was reminded of this last week when my youngest daughter, who is interning with an organization that helps to settle refugees, asked me to think of a skillset that inspires Americans to stereotype wealthy humans positively and those who live in poverty negatively.

"Speaking different languages," she said. "When wealthy people speak different languages, they're often viewed as intelligent and cultured. When poor people speak different languages, they're often viewed as ignorant and incompetent." And this struck a nerve with me.

Graphocentrism—the belief that those who know how to produce written words are somehow superior to those who do not—is alive and well inside of schools (Feliu & Farreras, 2016, pp. 140–141). It's fed by our tendency to privilege alphabetic text and print above all other modes of expression and our desire to repair rather than understand those writers who don't perform the way we and other writing and education experts might expect them to. Rather than taking a sociocultural perspective on literacy—one that takes into consideration the very different funds of knowledge and experiences that diverse learners bring to the table—we apply singular definitions of what it means to read, write, listen, and speak well (Donizeth Euzébio et al., 2010).

Whenever I invite writers to express themselves using whatever modes of expression and materials they prefer, what they create is often far more meaningful, beautiful, and distinct. That's because multimodal compositions are often reflective of the creator's culture, funds of knowledge, and identity (Llopart & Esteban-Guitart Moise`s, 2018). They allow them to share the whole of who they are in ways that are as comfortable as they are compelling.

Choice matters here. So does our attention to constraint. Recent work with young writers in my Studio reminded me of this all over again. After making stories with puppets and articulated mannequins, I was struck by how many of the details they incorporated into their compositions aligned with their earlier identity work. Had I forced them to use written words to create these stories, I doubt they would have developed these ideas well. They weren't ready to communicate those ideas with print on the first go. Those words came after. This took a bit more time, but their final written drafts were stunning, and all of the making that brought them to that place served as the perfect visual backdrop inside of their final products.

I've also realized that offering an abundance of prompts throughout that process gives writers a great deal of breathing room and the ability to reject some ideas without worrying that doing so will leave them nowhere to go. Asking a variety of questions allows writers to ignore those that they aren't interested in. They can turn their attention toward those that generate rich ideas and ignore those that aren't as useful. Sometimes, I lay all of the prompts in quick reach. If I know this will overwhelm them, I control the flow instead. For instance, I might place a single prompt inside of a learning center filled with small blocks, pebbles, and popsicle sticks: *Make me the place you were in the last time you giggled*, I might say. I might place that same prompt on a slide next to a few others as well: Make the place you were in the last time you cried, or make me the place you were in the last time you felt really loved. Do you sense the shifting weight of each of those questions? Can you understand how each question might resonate differently, depending on the writer receiving it? How would this be a different experience if I offered writers a list of ten different prompts to choose from? I am not certain that one of these approaches is necessarily better than another. It tends to depend on the writers in the room, and how my initial attempt engages them—or doesn't.

So, rather than rushing back into your classroom with tightly designed activities that intend to help writers quickly define and share who they are, I encourage you to take a step back instead. Extend invitations for students to explore who they are in a variety of contexts: personally, within their families, inside of their local communities and schools, on their teams, in their classrooms, and inside of the wider world, which needs them to show up as socially, politically, and culturally conscious human beings. Invite them to explore how their religion, race, gender, and abilities influence who they are. Make space for them to consider how others share certain elements of their identities, where differences exist, and how this adds dimension to the culture you're all creating together and the learning and work you do together. Our writing workshops can become spaces where writers are able to come to know themselves and one another in far more meaningful ways. They can become spaces where tensions are navigated with sensitivity and where hope and even healing can happen.

Building Trusting Relationships

Now that we've explored what it means to deepen self-awareness, you might be better able to appreciate why we must begin there if we're to situate multimodal composition inside of writing workshops well. How we approach this shift has everything to do with who we are as teachers and how we view who the writers we serve are and all that they can be. It's impossible to build truly trusting relationships with and among writers in the absence of self-awareness. In my experience, it's the sharing of who we are, how we're coming to know ourselves and others, and how these discoveries shape our engagements with one another that make or break our relationships with young writers. Trusting relationships are protected by healthy boundaries, agreements that are reached together, and a kind of interdependence that decenters teachers and makes conscious space for writers to define and negotiate their relationships with one another.

We can begin this work by trusting writers first and foremost. We can trust that they know what they want, what they need, who they are able to trust, and who they need to set wider boundaries or even limits with. We can trust that they are capable, eager to grow, and interested in serving others in their efforts to do the same—especially us. We can also trust that when young writers don't present this way, there are solid reasons for any resistance we might sense, and that often, those reasons have everything to do with previous learning or life experiences that harmed them.

The single most important thing I've learned about building trusting relationships is this: When I am sincere with writers about the fact that I am their student, and when I position myself this way in their company, trust begins to build. This might happen slowly at first—especially with writers who are deeply and appropriately skeptical—but it happens. At some point, a writer will do something unexpected, something that deviates from what most students assume my expectations might be. When I take care to respond by documenting what they do instead of correcting, something shifts between us. When I express my interest in the craft or design moves they're making or the work they're creating instead of judging, they realize that I value their contribution. And if I'm able to do all of that while maintaining a genuinely curious posture instead of maintaining my expert stance, I know that we might reach a pivotal point in our relationship. To be trusted, I need to trust. To build trust among writers, I need to model it for every individual, especially when they show up in ways that I didn't expect them to. When other writers bear witness to how I handle such divergences, they begin to realize that we're really in this workshop thing together. We all have different expertise to share, and we'll all be called upon to contribute in a just-right way. Just because I'm the teacher, this doesn't make me an authority on all that writing is or especially, who the writers in the room might be. I'm learning, like they are, and I'm grateful for and humbled by the lessons they're teaching me.

While many in my position encourage writing teachers to document their own learning, few do so with the same intentions that I typically share. Documentation forces me to define things that are making me uncomfortable in my writing workshops. Sometimes I've called these things uncertainties or tensions. Joanne Picone-Zocchia, someone I learned much from in the past, refers to these issues as the "stones in your shoe" (2008). She also took care to remind me that these problems I longed to solve were actually gifts, and they are. This reminds me to pull them closer every time I'd rather push them away. Documentation enables this.

As a documentarian, I recognize that my efforts are yielding less than ideal results. I define what it is that I need to understand better, and then I document everything I can about it as I plan and teach and reflect. Documentation is humbling for sure, but it also keeps me curious. It truly made me a life-long learner, and when I realized this, it was freeing. I don't have to have the answers—not for myself and not for you, either. I simply have to show up ready to be humbled, in service to my greatest teachers—the writers in our workshop.

If you're ready to learn more about documentation and perhaps, begin a small project of your own, you might appreciate the story that follows. The way we talk about writing with young writers can strengthen or undermine relationships. Here's what documentation taught me about that.

A Peek Inside My Practice

Devin is a maker. On the first day of our Studio sessions in the summer of 2021, he bopped into the room, placed his snack and water bottle on his table, and headed directly toward the front of the room where all of the loose parts were located. He began inspecting them thoughtfully, picking a few up, turning them over in his hands, and thinking a bit before he decided whether or not to return them to their proper piles. Not every writer behaves this way when they enter our workshop for the very first time. Some take their seats and wait for direction. Some hit those loose parts like they've never seen blocks or clay before, as if they were given some kind of golden ticket to enter our space and the materials would disappear forever by day's end. Devin was as patient as he was curious. I could tell that he was an experienced maker, and this made me wonder what he would do with written words.

He wasn't thrilled when I invited him to put down a bit of print a few moments into our building. He wasn't resistant either, but he preferred to keep making. He also preferred to talk about his ideas rather than stopping to tether them to a page. Instead, he turned to Juliette, another writer at his table, and he invited her to play inside of the scene he was building. Juliette recognized the setting right away, and soon they discovered a shared interest: Both of them loved the same series of books. Suddenly, Devin had a collaborative writing partner.

I studied them at work together throughout the week, taking notes, photos, and recording our exchanges. Devin wrote his story aloud, using materials to make and remake his setting, and then playing out each scene. His ideas changed shape as he continued to make his writing. He refined his thinking. He leveled up his vocabulary. None of this surprised me, because I've been a good student of children who make writing for many years now, and I also take great notes. This is what astounded me most: Devin began rehearsing whole sentences of his story and then, paragraphs and passages, aloud. As he did, he varied the rate of his speech, his tone, and his pitch. He wanted to engage Juliette and his classmates. He wanted to engage the teachers in the room. And this didn't seem to be attention-seeking in any way. It was as if he knew how wonderful his story was (and it was), and he wanted others to enjoy it, too.

I couldn't document this experience carefully enough. It reminded me, all over again, how little I understood about what writing was and how to teach it well. It reminded me how much I could learn if I simply offered young writers invitations and choices, space and materials, and the opportunity to teach me a thing or two.

Creating an Environment that Sustains Diverse Writers Through Diverse Processes

If you've never invited writers to describe and even draw their individual processes, I can't recommend this enough. I've shared this idea in earlier books, and I'm leading with it here because what emerges from this process is some of the most important data that could be driving your instruction. I'm uncertain how the writers you know and love will respond, and I'll be honest, each time I workshop this with a different group, the results are always inspiring. What I do know is this: If you can make space for writers to be the writers they truly are, the workshop that you create will likely serve them well.

In *Cultivating Genius: An Equity Framework for Culturally and Historically Responsive Literacy* (2021), author Gholdy Muhammad reminds us that literacy is fundamental to all other learning. While literacy is the cognitive act of reading, writing, and speaking independently, it's also criticality as well. Literate human beings aren't simply able to read and write to acquire new knowledge or skills. Literate humans are able to read, interpret, and influence complex realities. Literate humans, Muhammad reminds us, are better able to seek and achieve liberation.

When I think about creating workshop environments that sustain diverse writers through their diverse creationary processes, it's her words that return to me now. For instance, I wonder: How will this space that I'm creating and the learning that we do here help students discover something about themselves? How will it help them discover something about others? Are the materials, resources, texts, and tools representative of the writers who work here? Are they representative of those who aren't in the room or perhaps even a part of our local community? Whose voices should be elevated in this space, and why? How are we achieving this? Where are we falling short?

I wonder how the learning and work we do in workshop will serve students well beyond it. Here, I often find myself channeling Tricia Ebarvia, whose own work with young writers inspires so many. An advocate for bringing "writing in the wild" into our classrooms and workshops, she endorses Paul Thomas's suggestion that writing teachers focus on building genre awareness rather than relying on formulas (Ebarvia, 2016). This might include the investigation of the very forms that children seem to love most—puppet shows, animated shorts, cartoons, and funny memes. Stories, opinions, arguments, and informational texts come in all sorts of different packages now, and most of them are multimodal. Even our youngest writers and designers must learn how to make writing this way.

I also wonder if the workshop environment I've created holds space for writers to think and compose things that speak to their growing understanding of the relationship between power, oppression, equity, and liberation. What does it look like if I'm accomplishing this well? What does it look like if I'm doing more harm than good? And how do we build these specific literacies joyfully, inside of celebratory culture that doesn't hold young people accountable for solving problems they did not create or steadying their gaze upon the world's problems in a way that only serves to traumatize or retraumatize them?

There are several approaches I take that serve me well in my own efforts to create an affirming and culturally sustaining environment for writers. Each depends on co-creation, predictability, play, and a shared vision that evolves in response to what we learn about one another as the workshop finds its legs and eventually begins picking up speed. They include moves like those that follow.

- Beginning the year with identity work that is rooted in abundant questioning and responses that do not need to be shared with the room. This is deeply personal reflection and writing that attunes writers to their own interests, and especially their needs. Writers also know that they can skip questions, focus on those that interest and serve them best, or ignore these invitations altogether.
- Building a shared vision for our work together, and teasing out our individual and collective wishes and worries accordingly. From here, we formulate agreements about what we should be sure to do and take care not to do as we build our writing community.
- Seeking feedback from writers about how my efforts to serve them are helping or hurting. Anonymous surveys, tickets out the door, and quick reflective sessions at the start or end of a workshop session are helpful here. Taking action in response to what I learn is important, and so is taking care not to personalize feedback that feels more like criticism.
- Sharing my own worries, needs, struggles, and flaws. I take care not to burden students with these things but instead, share how I'm grappling with them, seeking solutions, or chasing new opportunities. I also talk with writers about my instructional intentions, the choices I'm making as a teacher, what seems to be working, what isn't, and what I might do differently, and why.
- Interrogating the books, materials, resources, and tools I'm offering writers. Contextualizing them in light of who the writers in the room may be, the values we share, the vision we have for our work together, and the kind of good we want to do in the world matters.

- Validating translanguaging and code-switching, helping other writers in the room understand what this is, how and why it's done, and why it's powerful is essential.

Instructional Support that Prepares Writers to Produce Real Things for Real Audiences that Appreciate Them

As I think about teaching inside of a contemporary writing workshop, I'm reminded that so much of what we've always done remains the same:

- We still need to offer long stretches of time for writers to compose.
- We need to structure our year, our units, and the lessons, routines, and rituals that frame each day in ways that are predictable.
- Assessments and the data they produce still matter.
- So do local, state, and national standards.
- Authenticity is still everything. Writers continue to create real things for real audiences that really appreciate them.

None of that is new. Here's what is: We need to approach all of that work in ways that serve culturally diverse writers who will be expected to compose multimodally if they're to be of any real influence once they leave our workshops. To that end, the recommendations below might make your workshop evolution a rewarding one for all. If skimming this list leaves your head spinning, know that I'll make a close study of each recommendation one short chapter at a time throughout the rest of this text. I've also included practical tools and guidance that can ease your beginning.

- Frame your entire year in a way that ensures writers will investigate, analyze, and create a variety of multimodal genres and/or subgenres, unit by unit. When I'm supporting primary teachers, we design learning experiences that are two weeks long around narrative, information, and argument writing. These experiences stretch to four or even six weeks in grades 3, 4, and 5. Here, we teach test writing as a genre, and we devote three weeks to this. These more experienced writers make the last ten weeks of the year their own, bringing a composition that they began in a previous unit to full completion by the end of the year. I'll walk you through the planning specifics in the chapters that follow.
- Take care to share multimodal mentor texts beside print-heavy models as you explore each genre or form. For example, mysteries are composed with written words across the pages of a short story

or novel. They're also illustrated across panels in comic books, audio recorded for podcasts, and performed on screens both large and small. Read, listen, and observe widely. Notice these genres at work in the world, and invite writers to do the same. You'll find some examples in the appendix materials, but don't stop there. Create your own collections, and invite writers to add to them.

- Begin by building a conceptual understanding of the genre at the start of each unit. Do this by inviting writers to identify those key concepts inside of familiar texts that they know well. It may make sense that you feature examples of the genre that are composed with written words during this early phase of your exploration, as this is how most writers have previously been taught to conceptualize most genres. Once they've acquired knowledge of these concepts within a familiar form, invite them to connect those concepts by exploring their relationships with one another. For example, you might ask who the main character is in a children's book you've shared on the carpet. Or, you could challenge argument writers to examine the relationship between evidence and claim in an opinion piece printed in your local paper. After you've helped them acquire these concepts using an alphabetic form, support their transfer of this newly acquired conceptual knowledge to their analysis of far less familiar models. A ballet performance might include a main character, for instance. Can your students identify who it is? How do they know? Artists often sculpt arguments. Infographics include many of the elements of print-centric informational writing. Acquiring, connecting, and transferring the conceptual knowledge of a genre or subgenre across increasingly uncommon or dissimilar forms inspires writers to conceptualize and create their own eventually. This mental model is one that helps writers and teachers alike organize their understandings in ways that support transfer. Conceptualized by Julie Stern, Kayla Duncan, Krista Ferraro, and Trevor Aleo, it's referred to as the ACT: The Learning for Transfer Mental Model (Stern et al., 2021, pp. 9–21), and it will be elaborated upon further in Chapter 4.

- Deepen your instructional toolkit. Rather than limiting your lessons to targets that attend to the production of written words alone, consider those that make for successful multimodal composition. I take a much deeper dive into all of this in Chapters 6 and 7, but Figure 3.2 provides an initial glimpse that invites connection and perhaps, comparison. To what degree are you already explicitly inviting writers to understand the design inside of their making and play? Which of these concepts are brand new to you and the writers in your workshop? Which of them remain hidden? One way we can legitimize multimodal composition is by acquiring and using its language, documenting its presence, and studying how it grows writers and writing.

◆ Assess and offer feedback on design as well as writers' craft, and prepare writers to do the same. You'll learn more about this in Chapter 7.

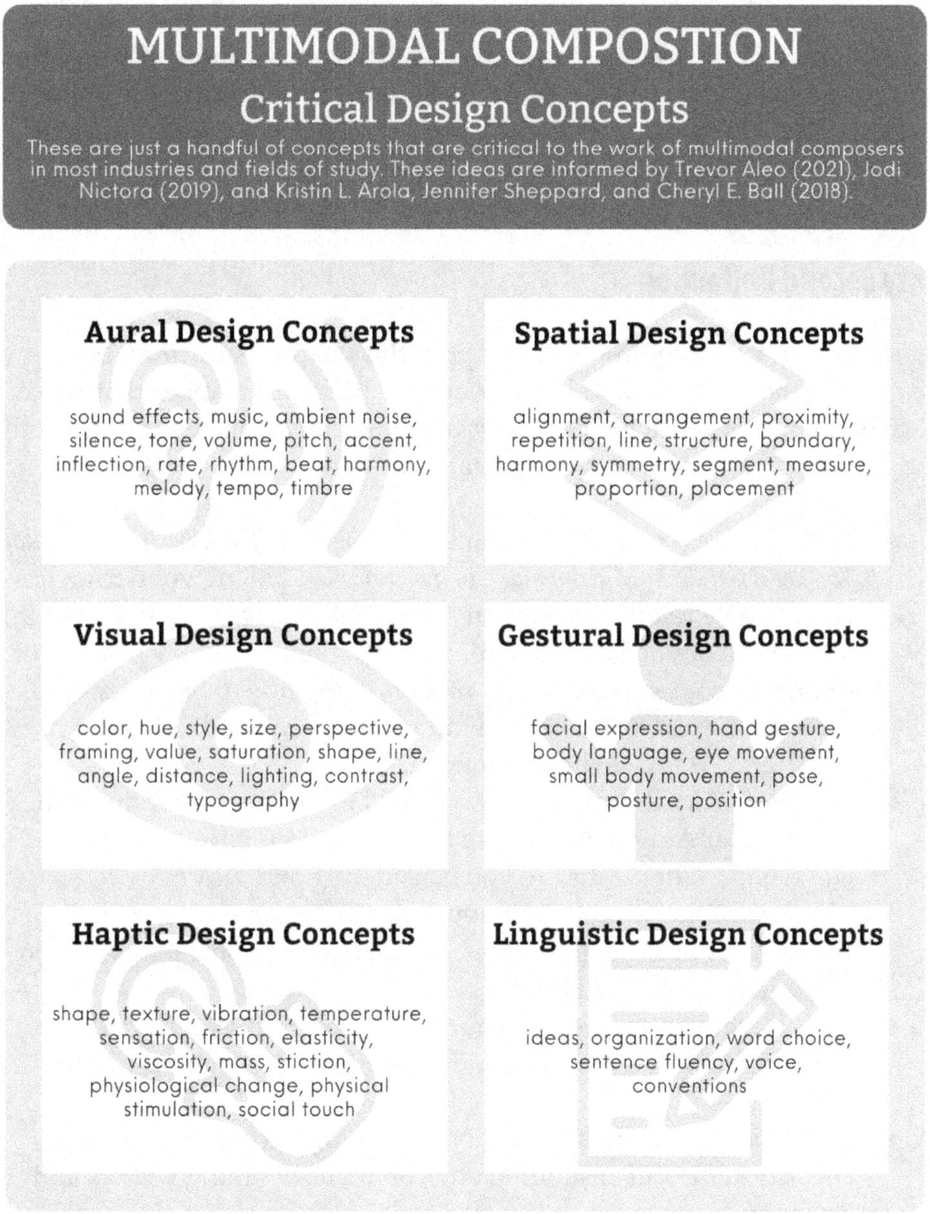

MULTIMODAL COMPOSTION
Critical Design Concepts

These are just a handful of concepts that are critical to the work of multimodal composers in most industries and fields of study. These ideas are informed by Trevor Aleo (2021), Jodi Nictora (2019), and Kristin L. Arola, Jennifer Sheppard, and Cheryl E. Ball (2018).

Aural Design Concepts

sound effects, music, ambient noise, silence, tone, volume, pitch, accent, inflection, rate, rhythm, beat, harmony, melody, tempo, timbre

Spatial Design Concepts

alignment, arrangement, proximity, repetition, line, structure, boundary, harmony, symmetry, segment, measure, proportion, placement

Visual Design Concepts

color, hue, style, size, perspective, framing, value, saturation, shape, line, angle, distance, lighting, contrast, typography

Gestural Design Concepts

facial expression, hand gesture, body language, eye movement, small body movement, pose, posture, position

Haptic Design Concepts

shape, texture, vibration, temperature, sensation, friction, elasticity, viscosity, mass, stiction, physiological change, physical stimulation, social touch

Linguistic Design Concepts

ideas, organization, word choice, sentence fluency, voice, conventions

Figure 3.2 Multimodal Composition: Critical Design Concepts

I hope you're beginning to recognize how you might reframe your workshop and recontextualize the curriculum resources you already use in service to this dynamic work rather than tossing things out or layering this kind of instruction on top of what you currently do. Whenever I'm invited to lead curriculum design work in schools, I'm sensitive to the importance of alignment and often, well-aware of the time and resources that have been invested in ensuring that each writer's journey through the system is as coherent as it is creative. I remain program agnostic, as much as possible. I also trust the teachers and administrators I'm privileged enough to support. The questions below may serve you well as you consider how to make the best use of the curriculum you're committed to, the resources that support it, and this call to redefine what writing is and how it is typically taught.

Sixty Second Reflection

Let's take a moment to process and apply this chapter's learning before we move on to the next. If you'd like a sounding board, remember that you can reach out to me on social media. I'm @AngelaStockman on Twitter, and you'll find me @angela_makewriting on Instagram.

- First, if you've read the companion to this text, *The Writing Workshop Teacher's Guide to Multimodal Composition (6–12)*, I'm wondering how what you've read here compares and contrasts with Chapter 3 in that text. Those of you who have read both are likely literacy coaches or leaders in your systems, and I'm wondering how this work might live within your K–12 world. Find me on social media if you'd like to talk more. I'd love to hear from you.
- How do the load-bearing walls defined in this chapter compare to those you already seem to have in place in your current writing workshop? What shifts are you considering and why?
- Which specific moves might you make to improve your current curricula, your use of resources, or your instructional plans? When will you make them? How?
- How might you reorganize your writing units, lesson plans, and resources in order to invite concept acquisition, connection, and transfer?
- How does this approach support your work to create a culturally affirming and sustaining environment for young writers and designers?
- How is your thinking, learning, or work continuing to change?

References

Donizeth Euzébio, M., Anderson, J. G., & Angelita, D. M. (2010). Literacy: A discussion of graphocentrism in microculture. *Fórum Linguístico, 6*(2), 39–53. https://doi.org/10.5007/1984-8412.2009v6n2p39

Ebarvia, T. (2016, September 27). Writing in the wild: Beyond the 5-paragraph essay [web log]. Retrieved September 12, 2021, from https://movingwriters.org/2016/09/27/writing-in-the-wild-beyond-the-5-paragraph-essay/.

Feliu, F., & Nadal Farreras, J. M. (2016). *Constructing languages : Norms, myths and emotions*. John Benjamins Publishing Company.

Holmes, J., & Wilson, N. (2017). *An introduction to sociolinguistics*. Routledge.

Lienhard, J. (1993). *Blueprint: Engines of our ingenuity* [Radio broadcast]. Houston Public Radio. https://www.uh.edu/engines/epi802.htm

Llopart, M., & Esteban-Guitart Moise`s. (2018). Funds of knowledge in 21st century societies: Inclusive educational practices for under-represented students: a literature review. *Journal of Curriculum Studies, 50*(2), 145–161. https://doi.org/10.1080/00220272.2016.12

Muhammad, G. (2021). *Cultivating genius: An equity framework for culturally and historically responsive literacy*. Scholastic.

Picone-Zocchia, J. (2008). Communities for learning: Leading lasting change summer retreat. West Cornwall, CT.

Stern, J. H., Ferraro, K. F., Duncan, K., Aleo, T., Hattie, J., & Zhao, Y. (2021). *Learning that transfers: Designing curriculum for a changing world*. Corwin.

Stockman, A. (2021). *Creating inclusive writing environments in the K–12 classroom: Reluctance, resistance, and strategies that make a difference*. Routledge.

4

Curriculum Design

I remember my first teaching evaluation. A newly minted teacher, I'd designed a writing workshop lesson down to its last detail. As these were the days before the miracle of Google Drive, that plan consumed 15 pages of printer paper, and that was before I designed my status of the class charts. I wanted my intentions to be clear. I wanted the alignment to be transparent as well. I wanted to impress my principal. Most importantly, I wanted my lesson to move the young writers in my class forward.

And it did.

So, imagine my surprise when, during our debrief, my principal suggested that I'd overplanned. "You've done fine work," he smiled reassuringly. "I just wonder how much room you've left yourself for learning while you teach. When plans are this water tight, I worry that teachers like you feel they must follow every precious letter. What if you simply stated your outcomes, defined your resources, and followed your daily workshop structure? What if you didn't think of every single question you intended to ask ahead of time? What if your assessment happened in the moment?"

My head was spinning.

This seemed antithetical to every single best practice I was taught to uphold as a pre-service teacher. It also seemed rather terrifying. I mean, anything could happen with that kind of planning. What if I didn't know how to respond? What if I wasn't ready for that? What if I lost too much control?

My principal, who likely felt my blood pressure rising from across the room, leaned forward with a gentle smile. "I might be a bit different than others who have evaluated you before," he admitted. "I'm not as impressed by the plans teachers create as I am by the moves they make as the lesson unfolds. I hope that they will plan well, but then, notice and reflect upon how students engage with those plans, or choose not to. I care less about the plan and quite a bit more about the way a teacher notices things that are unexpected and then shifts in response to them."

Yes, this principal was quite a bit different from others who had evaluated me before.

This memory returns to me each time I begin a new curriculum design experience with writing teachers in any school or district. I'm fairly experienced with curriculum mapping, and I've led curriculum design work in many different systems now. There are important nuances between those two different types of planning work. Curriculum design is a writing process that inspires creators to assume varied postures depending on their intentions and the people they're creating for. We design curricula for many reasons and for many different audiences. I've learned that when the modes, forms, and outlets we use to create and share curricula are chosen with intention and in alignment with that greater vision, the results are far more satisfying.

I didn't have this awareness as a young teacher or a staff developer. Those were the days when units, lessons, and grade level plans were universally mapped inside of spreadsheets, templates, or curriculum mapping software, mostly for alignment purposes. Our audiences were fellow teachers within and beyond our departments, administrators, and other stakeholders who had a vested interest in how our curriculum was articulated and aligned but who were not able to be in our company as we were designing or teaching it. Our plans needed to make the quality of our curricula transparent and easy to interpret and implement, even if we weren't the ones to do so. These were our greater priorities then, and facilitating this work taught me a great deal.

For instance, I learned that protecting time and space for divergent thinking and idea generation resulted in compelling learning experiences that we actually enjoyed making and learners enjoyed sinking into. I also realized that the parts of my work that attended to messier and more creative thinking were always sort of truncated because I knew that time was tight. I asked provocative questions and paired people together to brainstorm and hang ideas together, and some of that was useful to be sure. But, we relied on our spoken and written words exclusively as we moved through that quick brainstorming process, and we rushed toward whatever devices, platforms, or tools we were using to articulate our plans for the audiences who were expecting us to deliver them.

I never stopped to think about the writing process I was creating for myself or inviting teachers into, then. And when time was tight, I cut minutes and hours from the divergent thinking phase of the work in order to protect time for decision making, curriculum articulation, and data entry.

I know better now that it doesn't have to be this way.

Defining the Ways We Create Curriculum

It's interesting to me that we spend so much time inviting teachers to design engaging, multimodal, experiential, and authentic learning experiences for writers, but we don't often create processes that invite them to do the same. Instead, we usher teachers through the creative process, using tools that privilege print and alignment above all other modes of expression, in service to audiences who intend to evaluate their work. We sacrifice creative, empathetic design on the altar of alignment, and then we're surprised when teachers don't make use of the curriculum that they've invested so much time and energy aligning.

I was reminded of this in the spring of 2020 when the COVID-19 pandemic forced our rapid shift to remote learning. At the time I was facilitating curriculum design in several New York State school districts. We were mid-process, and some of the warnings I'd made early on in our work came rushing back to me. I wondered if teachers were remembering, too. I'd recommended that they design agile curriculum and that we not over-articulate too much, lest it become unwieldy. It was my hope that as they were making the transition to remote instruction and back and forth again, that they were able to lift, move, mix, and remix our frameworks with ease and without disrupting alignment. It was my hope that the experiences that they and their students were having alone, together, and alone together, were informing their instruction and that their curriculum frameworks held space for them to teach through the uncertainty in ways that were just-in-time responsive.

When curriculum is over articulated, making those kinds of moves can be a very difficult thing, and oddly enough, our tendencies to hyper-align curricula actually undermine alignment entirely. This is why, while I advocate for alignment on and across grade levels, I also remain keenly interested in the relationship between creativity and constraint and how different teachers within different systems moderate both. Only those who have great experience witnessing and negotiating those tensions in very different contexts can fully appreciate the intention that must be brought to the way curriculum is designed. I find that unless I invite teachers into an environment that is just as equitable, engaging and creative for teachers as the experiences we expect them to design for their students, it's almost impossible to sustain the work or what it ultimately produces.

Distinguishing curriculum mapping from curriculum design is helpful here. Each serves a different purpose, and the resulting products serve different audiences in different ways.

Fenwick English was the first to introduce curriculum mapping to the field (English, 1980). The purpose of such maps was to make clear what teachers were teaching and when they were teaching it. It was Heidi Hayes Jacobs who made mapping an instrumental process inside of most schools with the publication of her book, *Mapping the Big Picture: Integrating Curriculum and Assessment K-12* (1997). This is when teachers began keeping individual diary maps, sharing them with grade-level colleagues, and then, seeking vertical alignment in order to identify areas of repetition and gaps in their content, skills, assessments, and resources that were being used. Consensus mapping emerged from this as states began defining content-specific standards and disciplinary teams began interpreting and aligning their plans accordingly. Curriculum maps remain a powerful force inside of the alignment world, and mapping software and other digital technologies enable those who invest in this process to make adjustments in real-time and hyperlink relevant resources and tools in order to make their plans transparent and accessible.

Curriculum design is the process through which curricula are created. Good design is rooted in empathy work that ensures that learners' needs and interests inform how curricula are hung together by putting them at the table as the work is unfolding.

Good design serves the teachers who create the curricula well, too. The products remain important, and alignment is still essential here, but our understanding of how curricula are created and shared and who our audiences are during different phases of the work is a bit more expansive. For example, teachers might begin by investigating issues of importance to the learners they serve, taking photos, or documenting findings on sticky notes. They might study these notes collaboratively to identify emerging trends, and then, they might rapidly frame out a year using chart paper, additional sticky notes, and markers. These frames might be hung beside those designed by other teachers within or across different grade levels, and groups might physically gather around them to engage in collaborative analysis. Ideas might continue to be shared this way, and adjustments might be made by adding, removing, or replacing notes. Individual teachers might do similar work in their own sketchbooks or on charts in their own classrooms, where learners might contribute to their emerging plans.

While curriculum maps are documents or tools that are designed for those eager to investigate and study what is being taught and when, curriculum design is the process through which learning experiences are conceptualized, sketched, tested, and iterated upon using tools that support collaborative multimodal thinking and expression, fast drafting, and just-in-time revision. Maps are typically designed for those who seek clarity around curriculum plans. Design thinking invites teachers to collaborate with learners as they create, test, and improve these plans. Maps often require significant time and effort to create, and they privilege the use of written words. Design invites game-like play and a sort of experimentation that demands rapid prototyping, agile tools, and a much lighter lift. In my experience, the best maps emerge from quality design experiences.

The Essential Elements of a High Quality Curriculum Design Experience

High quality curriculum design experiences are as fortifying for teachers and their design teams as they are productive. While such experiences result in the articulation of high quality curricula, their value is far greater than this. For example:

- Such experiences invite teachers and students alike to deepen their self-awareness, express their interests and needs, practice empathy, and design in service to one another.
- While the alignment of content, skills, assessments, resources, and standards remains important, this alignment work attends to far greater vision that is co-created by teachers and students alike.
- High quality curriculum design experiences invite multimodal expression and composition. Products do not privilege print, and creators are not required to use digital technologies in order to articulate their plans. Those tools might be used to articulate alignment within and across grade levels, but that happens beside good design, not in place of it. The plans serve as vehicles for learning and agency building, and their primary audiences are the teachers and students who are learning how to collaboratively create them.
- Visual thinking is prioritized, as are the protocols, tools, and materials that support it.
- Designers deliberately cycle through divergent, emergent, and convergent creative phases that enable them to leverage incoherence and uncertainty in service to alignment.
- Designers actively seek diverse perspectives and high quality feedback from their colleagues and students and other experts in the field who live and work well beyond the boundaries of their own communities.

◆ Plans are tested quickly, and learners know that their feedback is an integral part of improving curricular design as well as instructional practice.

While my previous curriculum mapping and design experiences certainly invited some or even all of this work, I've struggled to establish frameworks and tools that make space for this kind of thinking, learning, and work. I'm still uncertain which of them might serve teachers and writers best, and that's why you'll see an assortment of options across different planning tools that I've left in the appendix. One thing is for certain: Curriculum initiatives that center frameworks and tools at the expense of creative design that intentionally supports learning transfer typically fail to deliver on their intended outcomes. This is why I've come to appreciate the ACT: The Learning for Transfer Mental Model (Stern et al., 2021, p. 10).

ACT: The Learning for Transfer Mental Model

A high quality curriculum framework articulates the compelling questions, concepts, content, skills, and assessments that learners will engage with as they move through a system. Each teacher within that system co-constructs the frameworks for their grade levels and disciplines with the students who will consume the curricula they articulate. Quality curriculum frameworks are detailed enough to make their intended learning experiences and processes transparent and coherent, but not so detailed as to constrain teachers and learners to tight pathways as they move through each day of learning together. Frameworks are expansive, agile, and ever-evolving. They define the load-bearing walls that ensure a quality curriculum, but they do so in a way that invites learners and teachers to rough-in each frame. This is essential when designing curriculum for a writing workshop that welcomes multimodal composition in particular because genre is a complex creature that shape-shifts in response to our purposes, the postures we assume, the audiences we're designing for, and the context our work will be shared within.

It's important that we design a coherent year of learning for the writers that we serve, and it makes sense to frame that year around specific writing purposes. For instance, writers might begin the year learning how to compose to inform or teach an audience about something they know a great deal about. Then, they might compose to share a compelling story. Their third learning experience of the year might involve crafting opinions or arguments intended to call their audiences to action. Additional experiences might invite writers to approach these same forms from a different perspective, or they might introduce entirely new ones. After much investigation, prototyping, and drafting, writers might end the year refining one of the compositions created during those previous experiences and launching it for an authentic audience. Defining the specific purposes or stances that writers will assume as they move from the beginning to the end of the year is a meaningful way to begin your own planning.

Next, consider how, as writers wade into each of these experiences, they will learn that a single genre assumes a very different aesthetic and form depending on a writer's intentions, what they hope to express, and who they hope to express themselves to. For example, one writer might compose a personal narrative across the panels of a comic book. Another might choose to use her blog to share her personal narrative instead. A third writer might podcast her personal narrative, while another classmate might make an infographic that reveals a timeline of turning points in her life and an audio recording that enables listeners to hear her story as they view this visual. Thanks to technology, these sophisticated forms are accessible to even our littlest and least experienced writers. Are you feeling daunted by these contemporary forms? I've left several different how-to guides for you in the appendix, including one that will guide you and your students through stop-motion video creation. Look for the Starter Sets there.

These compositions, which do not necessarily privilege written words, all contain the most essential elements of the personal narrative we've always known and loved. Multimodality challenges writers to choose their modes with intention, selecting those that enable the best expression of their messages and choosing their compositional materials and tools accordingly. The comic book, blog, podcast, and infographic all qualify as personal narratives because they contain the common elements and features that define the personal narrative. Each is a genre of its own as well, because each contains the common elements and features that distinguish comic books from blogs and podcasts and infographics. While very young writers and designers may not yet have these understandings, explicit instruction within our writing workshops will build it over time.

One might assume that this would demand the use of complicated curriculum frames and mental models, but this isn't the case at all. Skilled multimodal composers develop a level of genre awareness that deepens as we explore increasingly uncommon, dissimilar, and shape-shifting forms. For writers to become expert in this work, they must be able to define the organizational structure of the genres they wish to create as well as the concepts and features that distinguish it from other forms. They must be able to transfer these understandings to new and different forms as they emerge as well. Deepening learners' conceptual understandings of genres and forms enables them to notice their distinct characteristics or features inside of widely diverse examples. Young writers consistently surprise me with their capacity for this work. Accomplishing this requires a certain kind of planning though, and the ACT: The Learning for Transfer Mental Model, conceptualized by Julie Stern, Krista Ferraro, Kayla Duncan, and Trevor Aleo supports it well (Stern et al., 2021, pp. 5–22). Figure 4.1 demonstrates how we might apply it for our specific purposes as teachers who support multimodal composition.

During the ACQUIRE phase of the learning experience, writers acquire knowledge of single concepts within a specific genre by identifying them inside of several similar and familiar examples. For instance, writers might study how an author introduces a character at the start of several short stories that are composed of written words. They might also study how settings and problems are created inside of each story. Here, writers take care to distinguish examples of characters, settings, and problems from nonexamples of these concepts as well. They explain each concept in their own words, and then they MAKE each concept non-linguistically, using modes and materials other than written or spoken words (Stern et al., 2021, p. 10–14).

After writers have acquired knowledge of single concepts, they begin to CONNECT them to one another by noticing their conceptual relationships. "What does the setting teach us about the character?" we might ask. "How

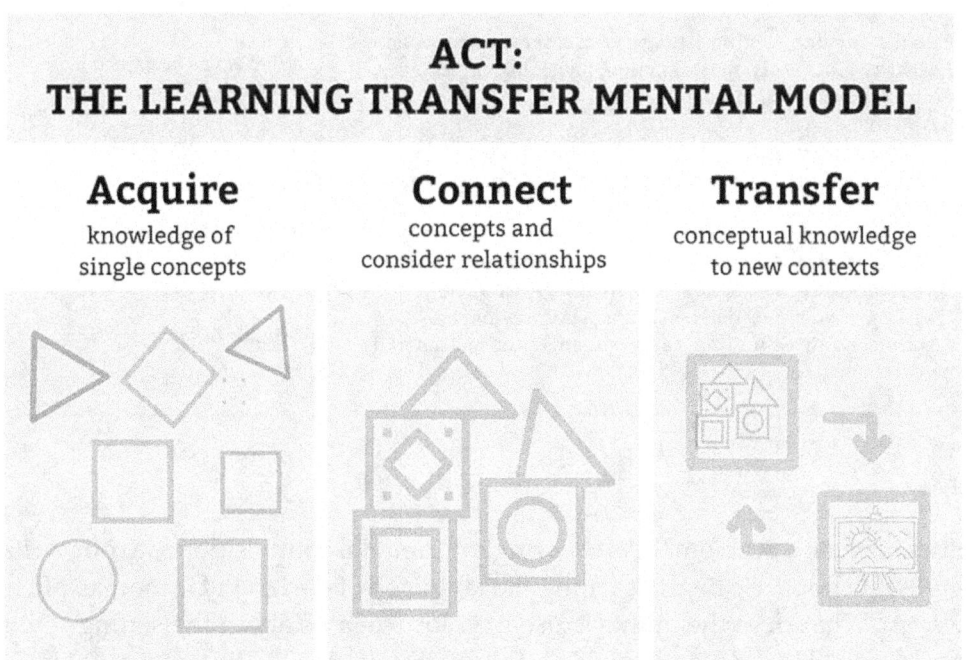

Figure 4.1 ACT: The Learning for Transfer Mental Model

QUESTIONING TO REVEAL CONCEPTUAL RELATIONSHIPS

Key Concepts

Aural Design:
sound effects, music, ambient noise, tone, silence, volume, pitch, accent, inflection, rate, rhythm, beat, harmony, melody, tempo, timbre

Spatial Design:
alignment, arrangement, proximity, repetition, line, structure, boundary, harmony, symmetry, segment, measure, proportion, placement

Visual Design:
color, hue, style, size, perspective, framing, value, saturation, shape, line, angle, distance, lighting, contrast, typography

Gestural Design:
facial expression, hand gesture, body language, eye movement, small body movement, pose, posture, position

Haptic Design:
shape, texture, vibration, temperature, sensation, friction, elasticity, viscosity, mass, stiction, physiological change, physical stimulation, social touch

Linguistic Design:
ideas, organization, word choice, sentence fluency, voice, conventions

The Rhetorical Situation and Elements of Form:
audience, purpose, context, plot, message, characters, setting, theme, conflict, resolution, claim, evidence, counterclaim, refutation, call to action, topic, facts, details

Question Stems

What is the relationship between x and y?

If you change x how does it influence y?

How does x enhance y?

What does x require of y?

How does x diminish y?

Is x necessary for y?

How does x align with y?

What does x afford us that y does not?

What would be lost if x did not exist with y?

What would be gained if we removed x from y?

When we vary x how does it change y?

How do we balance x with y?

How is x tempered by y?

What is the effect of x and y on z?

Figure 4.2

does it create a problem?" As we bring multimodal composition into our writing workshops, we begin teaching the language of design in far more explicit ways. "What does the author's use of color teach us about the setting?" we could ask. "How does the music influence the setting?" The conceptual relationship stems you see in Figure 4.2 are inspired by Julie Stern, Krista Ferraro,

Kayla Duncan, and Trevor Aleo, who introduce this approach in Chapter 6 of *Learning that Transfers: Designing Curriculum for a Changing World* (Stern et al., 2021, pp. 162–164). Offering them to the writers you serve will help them define and connect concepts within genres and across different forms. Know that this set isn't comprehensive. It's there to support and inspire your beginnings. You will find many more concepts to explore with writers as you learn more about crafting multimodal compositions.

Once writers have acquired and connected these concepts, they use their deepened understandings to analyze unfamiliar compositions and then plan to create their own. This is where TRANSFER occurs. According to Stern, Ferraro, Duncan, and Aleo, similar transfer invites writers to transfer the knowledge and skills they've gained in one context to another that is very much like it. Dissimilar transfer challenges writers to transfer the knowledge and skills they've gained in one context to another that is not at all similar. When we invite similar transfer, we help learners build and use schema that enables abstraction (Stern et al., 2021, pp. 18–20). This serves them well as we gradually acclimate writers to compositional contexts that are increasingly uncommon or dissimilar.

Teaching for transfer is an essential component of a writing workshop that welcomes multimodality. It makes sense then that our curriculum frameworks help us plan and articulate this process well. ACT is an agile mental model that guides the way we conceptualize each distinct genre study within a year and each lesson within each genre study. We might widen or tighten our planning aperture, but the model remains the same. It's as elegant as it is dynamic.

Situating Standards Within the Frame

The ACT: The Learning for Transfer Mental Model is also considerate of the standards, resources, and tools that you have at your disposal. Whether your system is one that works with a specific program or you've invested a great deal of time designing consensus curriculum maps with your colleagues, you do not need to spend an unreasonable amount of time and energy revising your alignment documents to make space for multimodal composition.

Invite writers to consume the genres that you expect them to produce, help them notice the elements that appear within those genres and across the many different forms that they might take, and then invite them to connect and transfer those concepts to increasingly dissimilar examples. This doesn't require anyone to remove critical texts, content, standards, or skills from your curriculum. Instead, we might reorganize and reframe them in ways that make them more meaningful, as Julie Stern often recommends.

For instance, I once taught a unit that was centered around the beautiful children's book *Trombone Shorty* by Troy Adams (2015). As we read together, my students learned much about the way that a story is structured. Had I known about the ACT: The Learning for Transfer Mental Model during my first iteration of this learning experience, I'm confident that my curriculum design would have better supported multimodal composition. I've redesigned this plan in recent years, and the most current version can be found in the document titled Using the ACT Model to Plan on https://angelastockman.com/resources-2/. Adams's text still enriches our study of narrative, but now, writers are invited to examine and create multimodal compositions before using their conceptual knowledge to begin creating a stop motion video of their own.

Writers acquire knowledge of narrative, character, problem, solution, setting, imaginary event, and sequence by noticing them at work inside of a familiar nursery rhyme: The Itsy Bitsy Spider. Then, they study them at work inside of increasingly less familiar, or dissimilar, forms, including a puppetry performance and a comic. Next, they begin to notice relationships between concepts by analyzing how they connect and influence one another inside of another familiar but far more complex text: Adams's *Trombone Shorty* (2015). They connect them inside of increasingly dissimilar multimodal forms as the learning experience continues to unfold, including an animated short and a piece of classical music.

As the genre study unfolds, writers acquire, connect, and transfer their conceptual understanding of narrative and its components across multimodal forms before beginning to develop their own. In this case, we made stop motion videos. You're welcome to use my resources and planning tools for this in your own work as well. I've left them in the appendix. Here's what I wonder, though: How might you use the ACT model to execute that portion of the learning experience? What might that look like?

I should take care to mention that many of the concepts I used for this particular plan were gleaned from the *New York State Next Generation English Language Arts Standards* (2017). As I reframed my original unit, I took care not to disrupt the original alignment to these standards. I simply rearranged the content and repurposed the resources. The ACT model elevated the complexity of this experience, illuminating the relationships between critical concepts and building schema that scaled across multimodal forms and more importantly, into new compositional contexts.

Hanging It All Together

As you begin to design or adapt your curricula, the planning tools in the appendix might inspire you as well. Here, you'll find varied examples to inspire you—some are composed in sketchbooks, others on foam boards or flip chart paper, and others are designed in Google Slides or on Canva. As you explore that resource, look for the invitation to access my Planning Camp podcast in the Welcome message on page 3. Listening might offer you just-right support as you dive into this work yourself. As you explore the models offered there, strive to identify the critical concepts at work inside of all of them. What do all of the planning models have in common? How do they differ? Which examples inspire you? Which ones might you call your own? How might you design a high quality curriculum framework that honors the very best of what you currently do while reframing it in a way that invites multimodal composition?

In recent years, I've codesigned curricula with different primary and intermediate level teachers using this approach. It helps us hang entire years of study together well.

- Writers move through multiple writing experiences in each single year. Each of those experiences builds an awareness of narrative, research and information, opinion, or argument writing. A variety of multimodal examples are explored, and writers work with teachers to define their distinct conventions. What makes a narrative a narrative? Which concepts are at work inside all narratives, regardless of the multimodal form they might take? We remain aware of this reality throughout this work: Genres are constantly changing shape, and when we invite writers to engage in multimodal processes that support multimodal products, feasibility becomes a critical consideration. For all of these reasons, it's important to seek conventionality and consider what's possible beside writers rather than simply teaching a predetermined set of rules that relate to only one particular form of any story, argument, or informational text beside a flipchart or white board.
- Writers typically define the structure of each genre by exploring these examples or mentor texts, and then, they use materials and modes of expression other than written words to make or perform their intentions for each bit of these structures. This enables us to assess the degree to which they have a viable plan for the whole of any composition. As I've explained in many different contexts within and beyond this book, I refer to this multimodal process as making writing (Stockman, 2015). This sort of play invites rapid ideation, design, and (my favorite) the use of sophisticated words and ideas that writers would not otherwise be able to access. If you'd like more explicit guidance for approaching this work in your own classroom, look for the Make Writing Starter Set in the appendix.

- Once we're certain that writers have a coherent plan and powerful intentions for each part of the structure, we begin teaching into that structure one small bit at a time. It's the structure of the genre that drives our lesson planning here. For instance, we might devote a week to just the beginning of a story. Each daily lesson might focus on a different writing skill relevant to this small part of the structure, and writers might use multimodal expression to deepen their design before transitioning to print. Would you like to see what this looks like? Explore the Planning Tools available for download on https://angelastockman.com/resources-2/.
- As we build each part of the story structure bit by bit throughout the week, we take care to document what we notice about each writer's use of spelling, punctuation, mechanics, and grammar. This informs the last lesson of each block, which focuses on conventions. For instance, before writers transition from writing the beginning of a story where a character is introduced to the next bit of their story where motivations are revealed, we will take care to teach and apply the conventions that they're in need of learning. This ensures consistent opportunities to deepen students' awareness of conventions without compromising flow or attention to the content they're creating.
- This approach also supports robust formative assessment that prioritizes process over product. Writers may not finish every piece, and that's okay. In fact, we might reserve time at the end of each quarter, semester, or year for learners to revisit the compositions they've started and bring one of their own choosing to completion.
- Time might be provided to writers to continue working on these compositions during other moments of the day, week, quarter, semester, or year as well. They might embrace the work they began within a unit as a passion project. They may also opt-out of the project entirely as they begin the learning and work of a new unit.

How might you apply a similar approach as you rethink the way you hang your own year together and move writers through it? The chapters that follow offer clear guidance here, but know that your own mileage may vary. This is one way to bring multimodal composition into our workshops and classrooms—it's not *the* way. If your process is different and it's also working well for your students, I'd love to hear from you. Come find me on Twitter @AngelaStockman.

Sixty Second Reflection

Before we move forward, take some time to reflect. What is resonating with you so far, and what seems to be a bridge too far? These questions can help you gain clarity and make meaningful choices about your own curriculum design approach.

- How do you distinguish curriculum design from curriculum mapping?
- What does your current process for pursuing either or both look like?
- How might ACT: The Learning for Transfer Mental Model serve you and your students well in these endeavors?
- Which approaches, resources, and tools might best support your curriculum planning?
- What additional help will you need? Where will you seek it?
- How is your thinking, learning, or work beginning to change?

References

Andrews, T. (2015). *Trombone Shorty*. Abrams Books for Young Readers.

English, F. W. (1980). Curriculum mapping. *Educational Leadership, 37*(7), 558–559.

English language arts learning standards. (2017). New York State Education Department. Retrieved October 21, 2021, from http://www.nysed.gov/curriculum-instruction/new-york-state-next-generation-english-language-arts-learning-standards.

Jacobs, H. H. (1997). *Mapping the big picture: Integrating curriculum & assessment, K–12*. Association for Supervision and Curriculum Development.

Stern, J. H., Ferraro, K. F., Duncan, K., Aleo, T., Hattie, J., & Zhao, Y. (2021). *Learning that transfers: Designing curriculum for a changing world*. Corwin.

Stockman, A. (2015). *Make writing: 5 teaching strategies that turn writer's workshop into a makerspace*. Times 10 Publications.

5

Assessing Multimodal Processes and Products

The assessment mess. You know what I mean, don't you?

I've never met a writing teacher who wasn't well acquainted with it. The assessment mess confounded me throughout my teaching career, and much to my disappointment, stepping out of the classroom and into my role as a professional learning facilitator only increased this tension. Rather than grappling with it alone, I found myself in the company of quite a few other teachers who were crumbling under the weight of their nightly paper load and frustrated by the fact that their students weren't even reading let alone responding to their feedback. And it was my job to facilitate solution-finding.

Assessment was what made my first years of teaching the most uncomfortable, and if I'm being honest, it's the part of my learning and work that remains most uncomfortable for me now, nearly 30 years later.

Like many if not most of you, I grew up inside of a school system that valued products, the evaluation of them, and the grades that both produced. Little attention was paid to the writing process, and I received very little feedback on my writing until I was a freshman in college. Writing was assigned by my teachers. I completed those assignments, and then my teachers scribbled a few comments in the margins and gave me a grade. I absorbed the grade and tried to do better next time. Mind you, I wasn't at all clear about what better would look like, but I'd try.

It took many years for me to realize how formative those experiences were. They shaped me as a writer and a teacher. As it happens, trying to do better meant becoming an English major and learning how to craft better work. It also meant earning my teaching certification and trying to do a better job of assessing and feeding young writers forward. We teach the way we were taught, and my experiences as a young writer created biases that were difficult to recognize, particularly as a fledgling teacher who worked in systems that functioned very much like those I grew up within.

I continue to work in systems whose community and school leaders maintain very similar assessment perspectives and practices. It isn't until we know better that we're able to do better, and in my experience, the demands of doing absorb most of our time as writing teachers. Deepening what we know is a luxury, and few of us can afford to make that investment unless our mentors and leaders free up the space and time for us to do so.

If any of this resonates with you, I hope this chapter offers practical solutions. We each have our own assessment messes to contend with, but every time I invite a writing teacher to spill theirs on the table, I recognize the sharp edges of each ill-fitting element in their systems and the tangled knots that seem to twist the entire menagerie together. And that's before I even whisper an invitation to include multimodal composition in the mix. Assessment feels even slipperier in this context. Let's try to get a better hold on all of this. I know that if we don't, the likelihood of writing teachers welcoming multimodal composition into their workshops may be pretty slim.

Curriculum, Assessment, and Instruction Work Hand-in-Hand

By now, you likely understand that writing is not merely the production of written words alone, and that in fact, when we invite writers into a multimodal process that results in multimodal products, we're often better able to assess their strengths and gain far better perspectives about their needs. It isn't necessarily grading, but rather documentation, that supports assessment, reflection, and growth (for writers as well as teachers).

For instance, rather than waiting on writers to produce polished works so I can grade them, I'm able to collaborate with them as we make a shared investigation of their progress toward specific learning goals or targets each day. I use the word investigation with intention here. It supports the notion that assessment is a verb—it's a study that teachers and learners conduct together. It doesn't require us to pause learning in order to produce results, but instead, it empowers us to seek evidence of learning inside of the process and document our findings without disrupting it. When writers and teachers document not only the degree to which daily learning targets are met, but how this happened, everyone involved in the process becomes increasingly self-aware of their strengths, needs, and goals. This enables everyone to define productive next-steps.

Documenting what I'm learning about how writers are progressing toward the targets we've prioritized might inform what I will teach next, how I will teach it, and who will be included in specific lessons. When writers document their learning, they become better attuned to their interests, intentions, and the knots in their thinking and work. This makes their conferences with me and the support they seek from other writers much more meaningful and rewarding. The data that we gather from our documentation work together can be used for reporting purposes as well. I'll speak to this more shortly.

As Figure 5.1 demonstrates, documentation shines unfiltered light on our curriculum, instruction, assessment, and attempts to serve student agency. Historically, systemic efforts to move writers forward treat each of those domains as disparate entities rather than unifying and interdependent forces

Figure 5.1 Centuring Documentation Inside of the Writing Workshop

that help everyone gain traction inside of a messy and complicated process. We may speak about this relationship often, but when I'm invited to facilitate this work in schools, we typically have time to focus on just one of those elements, and as each initiative is completed, it's difficult to inspire teachers and leaders to sustain their learning and shift postures inside of their work. In many ways, we're just as product-oriented in our professional development approaches as we are in our writing workshops, and while grades aren't given, this mindset does just as much—if not more—harm. I know this because people like me are the ones perpetuating this problem, and while I've yet to enter a system that is fully healed, and I certainly have much more work to do myself as the designer of strategic plans and theories of change, I am confident that documentation offers solutions that few who are not committed to this work understand. Even small documentation efforts build strong connective tissue between what we teach, how we teach, how we assess, what we discover, and why.

A Peek into My Documentation Process

We had opened the day with an exploration of opinion writing. We'd studied how writers and designers share their opinions in picture books, through poems, in explainer videos, and through a raucous dance performance. The kindergarteners I was working with were ready to share their opinions. Some were building with LEGOs while others were using clay. A few were drawing. Just a few were making puppets and preparing to perform.

And I began to document what I was learning. Here's how:

- As I walked the room, I kept my learning target at the front of my mind: *We can use materials to share an opinion about something that matters to us.*
- As I visited each writer, I asked them to share what they were making.
- I also asked them to share how their creation revealed an opinion about something that mattered to them.
- Then, I asked them to tell me more about the materials they chose, why they chose them, and how they were helping them express their opinions.
- I used my phone to scoop and curate the most critical bits of data from these exchanges: photos, audio recordings, and quick video clips. Each of them aligned with the target above and my inquiries.
- I also used a mastery scale, much like you see in Figure 5.2, to document the degree to which each writer met the day's learning target.

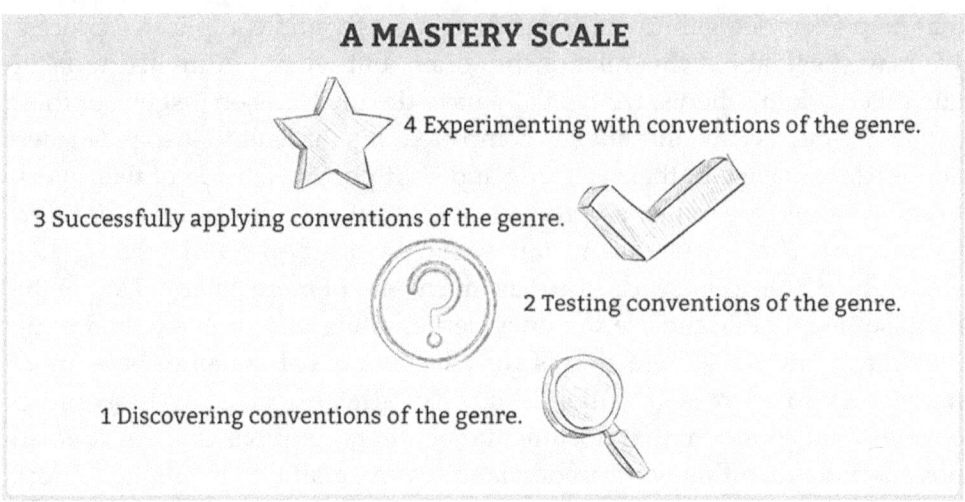

Figure 5.2 A Mastery Scale

Documentation allows us to gather frequent data from our own lived experiences and those of the writers we serve, in an effort to understand what is happening, what isn't, and why. This kind of assessment inspires teachers to value process and growth over compliance and performance. More importantly, it empowers writers to do the same. It also protects time and space for multimodal expression and composition, and this is critical.

This approach thrives inside of systems where competency-based learning or standards-based grading are the norm. It focuses our vision and targets our assessment so we're better able to help writers find clear pathways forward. What we learn informs how we teach, the feedback we provide, and how we define and measure success.

This approach also thrives inside of systems that still value grades and grade reports as well. Those systems may remain hard to dismantle, but documentation ensures they do less harm. It makes for far better decision-making, too. Let's examine how that might work.

Documenting to Do Less Harm

I've spent much of the last decade facilitating the shift to standards-based grading and reporting inside of various school systems. While many are initially inclined to rapidly redesign their report cards and begin employing a mastery scale, fewer appreciate the importance of shifting assessment practices first. In my experience, when teachers fail to establish good habits of documentation and a system that supports this kind of data collection, the reporting system ultimately fails to serve anyone well at all. In fact, changing the report card without changing some very essential assessment and reporting practices can actually do more harm than good.

Assessment is about uncovering the strengths and needs of learners, so that we might serve them better. Reporting is about making those discoveries transparent to children, their caregivers, and other decision-makers within our system (whose primary goal is to serve those same learners well). To accomplish this, the data we gather must be far more than robust—they must be exceptionally *revealing*. Quantitative data—the numbers we generate and analyze when we're studying student performance—rarely illuminate the root cause of any writer's strengths or needs. They cast a bit of light, but they also throw shadows. So too do many of our assessments and the way we document our findings inside of gradebooks, on progress reports, and on report cards.

Documentation makes us far better diagnosticians. Rather than waiting on your system to change, here's how you might begin to leverage it inside of your own writing workshop or classroom now.

- ◆ Target each day's learning, and make that learning target clear for your students. I might begin by helping writers understand that by the end of a day's session, they should be able to say, "I can use materials to build an opinion about something that matters to me."
- ◆ Teach and assess in small doses. For example, I might invite writers to explore how a variety of writers and designers do the same, in their own work. We might study how children's book writers or illustrators share their opinions using words and images. We might study how opinions are shared in podcasts made especially for children. We might tease an opinion out of a video advertisement. We might find one in an animated short. As we investigate the way that opinions are made and shared, we might discuss the multimodal differences and affordances. "What does video allow us to do?" I might ask. "What makes audio an interesting choice? Can you find the opinion in this illustration? How did the artist do that? Why do you think they made that choice?"
- ◆ Invite multimodal composition. "How will you share your opinion?" I might inquire. "Will you build it? Paint it? Act it out? Which materials or tools will you use?"
- ◆ As writers make or perform their opinions, document what you see and hear, in alignment with the target. Take photos, record a bit of audio or video, or make some notes. Even better—invite writers to do this themselves.

- Then, study what writers have produced and apply the mastery scale. To what degree are they meeting the target, using multimodal expression? Make note of this.
- Finally, invite writers to transition to print. Some might label everything in their build. Some might watch their video recorded performances or listen to themselves speak what they intend to write via audio recording. Others may move directly from making and performing to producing print.
- Study what they've produced again and apply the mastery scale. To what degree are they meeting the target using written words? Make note of this as well, and mind the gap between this performance and their last, the one they composed multimodally. What does this reveal about the writers in your room?

I've left a bit of documentation from my own experiences with young writers in the appendix and at https://angelastockman.com/resources-2/, beside my reporting tools. There, you'll see what I noticed, how I documented the learning writers made visible to me, and how I reported this information to others. Let's explore that a bit further.

Grading and Reporting

Most of the teachers that I serve still work in schools that rely on the same sort of report cards we've always used, and even those that are in the midst of shifting to standards or competency-based grading still find themselves grappling with reporting systems, tools, and practices that simply don't function as they could and should be, in service to young writers. These are still new and perhaps tenuous conversations for far too many people, and while I'd love to just tell everyone to ditch grades and do better, I know from experience that everything is a bit more complicated than that.

Here's an idea that you might find useful if you're living the same reality that I am many are living: Design learning experiences that deepen genre awareness one investigation at a time. Define the skills that writers will strive to master as they acquire and then apply what they've learned about creating such genres themselves. Document the degree to which learners have mastered those skills day by day, as you walk the room, peek into their work, and quickly confer with them. Use the mastery scale in Figure 5.2 to do this meaningfully and efficiently, distinguishing their multimodal performance from what they can do with written letters and words. Alternatively, you might also design one that aligns to your system's expectations in collaboration with your colleagues and the writers you serve.

Even if you're unable to document each writer's progress toward every target every day, the fact that each standard is composed of multiple micro-targets and students make several passes at them as they move through any investigation and writing experience ensures that you will be gathering much more evidence of students' learning than you would if you were simply grading the products of their learning. You also won't need to disrupt their creative process to accomplish this. This is work I've led in multiple schools and districts, and while it requires a commitment and significant change, it's one that results in far more meaningful assessment work, and ultimately, this is an effort that changes workshop culture for the better.

This approach honors the whole of who writers are and the complexities of multimodal composition as well. Assessment is about studying progress toward standards defined by each writer's investigation of the genre they wish to create as well as those standards we're mandated to pursue by the systems we teach within. This is very different from grading—a process by which we evaluate and score the products of learning.

While it's important to make an assessment of the final compositions that writers create, I encourage you to study their progress throughout the process as they make and write, bit by bit. This evidence can be used for reporting purposes, as long as we take care to use it as equitably as possible. We can accomplish this by relying on mode rather than averaging grades. Compare what you see in the Documentation and Reporting Sample (available at https://angelastockman.com/resources-2/) to your current assessment and grading practices. How might you make a similar shift?

And What About Report Cards?

When it comes time to translate your documentation into a grade, I recommend that you begin by looking at the dimensions of your report card with your colleagues and reaching agreements about where your findings might fit. For instance, you might notice that you've made many detailed assessments of learning targets that align to narrative writing in a single quarter. You might report these findings within the writing dimension of your report card. Or perhaps, your card is broken down into specific genres, and narrative writing is included in that mix. If this is the case, you'd report your findings there. Perhaps your report card generalizes even further, and you need to make a report of what you've noticed about your students toward reading, writing, listening, and speaking standards and you must do that inside of a dimension that is simply called English or English Language Arts. If this is the case, you will need to balance your assessment thoughtfully, and again, in collaboration with other colleagues who are reporting findings about writers who are taking the same course under their guidance. Understanding the relationship between standards, their sub-skills and associated learning targets, and the language of your report card is important here, and it varies from one system to the next.

Framing Better Feedback

According to John Hattie (2009), feedback has a significant influence on the quality of learning and progress that writers make, and what's more compelling is that it's the feedback that teachers receive from learners that seems to have the greatest influence. When writers and designers make their learning visible to us, and when we invest ourselves in seeing and hearing this learning, we offer better feedback. Other factors of importance include aligning our feedback to learning goals and ensuring that it is actionable and acted upon (Hattie, 2009, pp. 173–178).

As a young writing teacher, I struggled to provide high quality feedback on the written words that students produced. Decades later, I've gained so much more instructional experience, and I've evolved as a writer myself, but still, offering just-right feedback remains a challenge. I'm guessing that it might be one for you, too.

Learning targets are useful here. If I know what my target is, I can anticipate how writers might pursue it, and I can begin to move my brain up and down a scaffolded set of feedback frames and strategic craft moves that might help different writers who are in very different places meet that learning target well.

Feedback frames were very useful to me as an inexperienced writing teacher, and I continue to develop them for myself and in the company of other writing teachers today. You may have a wonderful selection of similar frames at your disposal. I've left others—including those that might help you talk with writers about design decisions—in the appendix. Don't limit yourself to these offerings. Create a process through which you might be able to frame high quality feedback yourself.

Begin with your learning target, and then reflect: What does it look like when a writer is doing that well? What does it look like when they're approaching that target but not quite there yet? And what does it look like when they're just gaining an awareness of what that target even means?

How might you frame your feedback in a way that honors where the writer is while illuminating different paths forward? How might you include them in defining and negotiating that path as well? If you've situated their writing experience inside of a greater investigation, as I've suggested, then writers will have learned a great deal about what "good" looks like through their investigation of different multimodal mentor texts. You don't have to be the authority here, and I encourage you not to position yourself this way. Learn from the writers you serve. Let them show you what a quality product looks like, and consider creating a checklist together. Then, use the checklist to define where the writer is in relation to each criteria, and frame the writer's next steps accordingly, and collaboratively.

The beautiful thing about positioning ourselves as collaborators is that it puts us in closer relationship with creators. Investigations make writers the experts in the work, and when we trust them to teach us about their intentions, it builds their confidence. It also builds their trust in us.

Sixty Second Reflection

Take a moment to reflect on all you've learned about assessment, grading, and reporting in this chapter. While you may not take swift action to shift everything about your practice now, questions like these can help you determine what must be done immediately and what can wait.

- How might you design your year, each unit, and your lessons in ways that invite multimodal composition ahead of the production of written words?
- How will you shift your grading and reporting practices in ways that better serve all writers?
- What pushback may you encounter? How will you respond? Whose support might be beneficial here, and how might you seek it?
- How is your thinking, learning, or work continuing to change?

Reference

Hattie, J. (2009). *Visible learning: A synthesis of over 800 meta-analyses relating to achievement*. Routledge.

Part 3

How Do We Teach Multimodal Composition?

6

Mentor Texts, Planning, and the Essential Elements of a Multimodal Composition

When COVID-19 came rolling into western New York, I decided it was officially time to take my show off the road for a spell. Having spent most of the last 15 years on planes, trains, and inside of rented automobiles consulting all over the country and inside of a few others, I knew that the pandemic would soon be compromising those opportunities for the foreseeable future. I also knew that as much as I loved working with the teachers that I got to meet on the road, I was longing for a professional home of my own.

I was fortunate to land a job as an instructional designer for Daemen College in Amherst, New York. I was also fortunate to receive the support I needed from leaders there to continue consulting in K–12 schools in whatever limited capacity COVID-19 would allow me. Two years later, I spend one week of every month designing fabulous learning experiences with writing workshop teachers and the remaining three on my campus, supporting instructors with course design, teaching my own classes, and growing my Make Writing Studio for K–12 writers and teachers. I know what a privilege all of this is. This doesn't mean that I don't encounter challenges nearly every day.

For instance, a few weeks ago, I found myself frustrated over the fact that no matter how many workshops, webinars, or asynchronous learning opportunities I put together, few of the instructors that I serve were able to participate. It wasn't because they weren't interested in professional learning—I know the level of scholarship that all of them pursue. They're committed learners. I also know that many of them, in fact, share my professional interests. So, what was up? I wondered.

DOI: 10.4324/9781003216940-10

Coincidentally, that same week, I began sharing small bits of that same webinar and workshop content inside of very different spaces, including Twitter and LinkedIn. I started a newsletter. I made quick videos and screencasts. Audio recordings. One-pagers. I shared them whenever instructors reached out to me by email or scheduled one-on-one consultations. I added them to a digital toolkit. I mentioned them in passing, at the cafe. And people started engaging. It wasn't hard to understand why: Time is tight, stress is high, people need just-right and just-in-time support, and multimodal content is engaging.

The same is true inside my wider learning network as well. I've published a few books, but I'm fairly certain that there are many more people who were moved to bring multimodal composition into their own classrooms by what I've shared on Instagram, Twitter, or Facebook over the years. People appreciate the content I drop into their inboxes each Sunday morning via my email list. They like the demonstration videos I post on YouTube and the peeks into my own writing studio that I leave in Google Photo albums that everyone can access whenever they like. This content is quicker to consume but no less meaningful. It also shows up serendipitously at times. I pay attention to when people are online, when they check their email, and when they're more likely to have five minutes to sit with something I've created—over coffee on an early Sunday morning, perhaps.

When I was a young professional, my mentors spoke to me about networking. They encouraged me to build relationships with those I admired in my field, to support their work, and to learn from them as well. Those charismatic souls who were able to light up every room they walked into had a certain edge here that others did not, and I can't help but notice how this phenomenon plays out in our current and much more digitally connected world. People's expectations have changed quite a bit since 1993. Today's professionals understand that in order to communicate effectively, they must use diverse media, multiple modes, and genre awareness to craft content that is culturally and socially expected in different situations (Arola et al., 2018, p. 60). That landscape is constantly evolving, too.

And I still have so much to learn about what it means to be a powerful writer these days, but wow, am I having a ton of fun experimenting and noticing things along the way.

For instance, I know that it's not enough to send administrators a lengthy written summary of the professional learning work I've facilitated in their districts recently if a video carries a message better. Newspaper advertisements don't perform as well as Instagram campaigns might. This depends on the season or even, the moment. My last professional collaboration was the result of a tweet. TED Talks were game changers long ago, and TikTok is a powerful platform for writers today. Understanding who hangs out where and what they are currently looking to consume is essential to developing audience awareness now. Learning how to create that kind of content with careful intention is the work of today's young writers.

So, who is teaching them how to do this well?

You are. You—the teacher who offers kids markers, construction paper, and clay. The one who takes your students outside to make shadow stories on the sidewalk. The one who makes space for imaginative play and art centers. Puppet shows. Dance performances. If I'm being honest, I've never worried much about whether or not young writers and designers were well supported in primary and elementary schools. I've worried quite a bit about what happens after grade 4 or 5 though, when all of those opportunities seem to dwindle or disappear entirely.

I hope this validates any current efforts you're making to invite multimodal composition into your own writing workshop—whether you teach kindergarten or third or fifth grade. The writers in your room may not yet be composing sophisticated websites, interactive apps, or polished podcasts just yet, but there is one thing I'm certain of: If they don't have ample opportunity to make, perform, and play their way through the writing process in elementary school, they won't feel comfortable let alone confident in their abilities to do so once they reach middle or high school.

Explicitly teaching the essential elements of multimodal composition might further prepare them well for this kind of writing and learning. It's not enough to create the space or the opportunity to write and design. We need to begin building a shared language for multimodal composition, and we need to pose questions that inspire even our youngest and least experienced writers to make and write with intention.

How might you do this?

The Essential Elements of a Multimodal Composition

It took some time for me to understand the relationship between the essential elements of a multimodal composition and how I might teach them—explicitly and coherently—inside of my own writing workshops and the classrooms I teach within. The possibilities are limitless of course, and that used to incapacitate me as I planned. Perhaps your experience is the same. Frameworks like the one you see in Figure 6.1 center me now, and they help me gain traction as an instructional designer.

Distinguishing audience, stance, modes, forms, and outlets from one another helps me situate them in relation to one another as I'm planning.

THE ESSENTIAL ELEMENTS OF A MULTIMODAL COMPOSTION

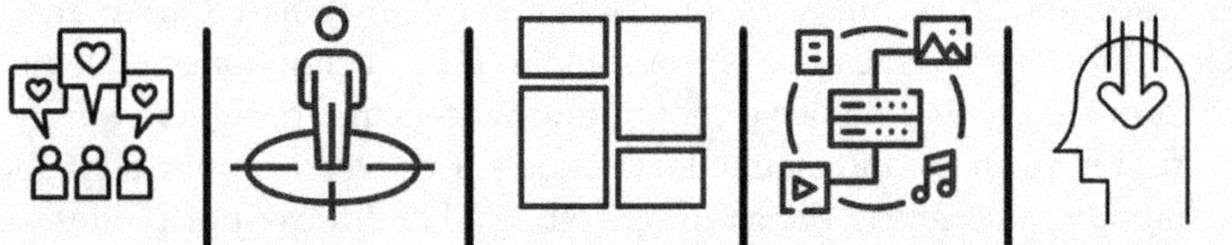

audience	stance	form	modes	outlet
Readers	Argue	Comic	Alphabetic	Website
Viewers	Persuade	Infographic	Visual	Blog
Listeners	Inform	Photo story	Gestural	Newspaper
Users	Call to action	Logo	Spatial	Magazine
Visitors	Empathize	Skit	Haptic	Twitter
Consumers	Serve	Stop motion video	Aural	Board Meeting
Clients	Disrupt	Zine		Celebration
Patrons	Entertain	Puppet show		Gift

Figure 6.1 The Essential Elements of a Multimodel Composition

You may not use this same language with the writers and designers in your workshop, but charts like these can help you and perhaps more experienced elementary writers make a meaningful analysis of multimodal mentor texts, tinker and play with different possibilities as creators, and make thoughtful predictions about how different choices will influence the whole of a composition as well as the audiences who will eventually receive it.

Kindergarteners may not be ready to think as strategically about these elements as fourth or fifth graders may be, but all young writers benefit from learning the language of multimodal composition. It's a bit more expansive than the one we speak when we're referring to the production of written letters and words alone.

Audience

Our audiences are the readers, viewers, listeners, users, and consumers of the compositions we create. Our relationship is a very human one wherein we strive to influence them through our work. How this happens has everything to do with each audience member's experiences, perceptions, values, and opinions. Understanding how the compositions we create might affect our audiences requires a depth of self-awareness that many young writers are just developing, and this is one of the primary advantages of bringing multimodal composition into our writing workshops: Just as each mode of expression affords writers something that other modes do not, the modes that writers choose to use bring their ideas to various audiences with varied effect. The process of creating multimodal compositions has the potential to deepen each creator's self-awareness if those who are guiding the process create space for this to happen. This is the same space that's necessary for thoughtful design work.

When we consider audience, we ask ourselves questions like these:

- Who am I making this for?
- What do I know about them?
- What do they care about?
- How can I get to know them even better?
- How will this help me make something especially perfect for them?
- How can I connect to my audience through my work?

Meet Shirel. An elementary writer in my Make Writing Studio, she'd decided early in our work together that she wanted to make a puppet show, but she didn't seem particularly excited about the prospect until I told her that we would be opening her show up to the entire community and that visitors from outside of our little studio would be joining us to watch her performance.

Who would be attending? We wondered. How could we be sure to make a show that truly entertained them?

Rather than simply flinging our doors wide open and waiting until the day of the event to learn who her real audience would be, Shirel decided to create a survey that every registrant would complete long before opening day. There, they revealed the titles of their favorite books, television shows, and films. Shirel wasn't aware of some of them, so she asked other studio members to help her get a sense of what these different stories were all about and what kinds of characters and life lessons readers and viewers met inside of them. Then, she crafted a puppet show that complemented their interests.

Stance

A writer's stance has everything to do with their intentions, perspective, and purpose. When young writers and designers consider the stance they will assume within their work, they explore questions like these:

- Why do I want to make this?
- How will it make others feel?
- What will it make others think about?
- How will it help the people who read it, watch it, listen to it, or play with it?

Surveying her potential audience helped Shirel choose a very intentional stance as a puppet show designer. She knew that she wanted to make her audience laugh because most of them loved funny stories about sweet characters. She also knew that she wanted her audience to think more about the importance of caring for elderly people. She hoped her puppet show would inspire people to invite their aging family members and friends to do something silly with them, so they could laugh together. The more thought Shirel gave to just those four questions above, the more clarity she gained about what she would create, how, and why. The greater her clarity, the more her enthusiasm for the project seemed to grow.

Form

Form refers to the shape, configuration, and conventions of a particular composition. Examples include posters, stop motion videos, sculptures, riddles, infographics, cartoons, comics, video games, poetry, puppet shows, and explainer videos. Some use the terms form and genre synonymously, and I understand this reasoning. For our purposes here, I prefer to speak to form specifically because historically, the way we've defined genre within the field of writing instruction speaks specifically to the configuration of written words alone, even though genres shapeshift in response to the needs and interests of different cultures, groups, and individuals. Genres also blend inside of most compositions. Stories are arguments. Information is shared through narrative. Poetry is research and information writing.

Genre has always been far more multimodal and messier than the way we tend to define it in schools, and because we've defined it so narrowly, using that term in the context of this work might be limiting. Form seems a far more inclusive term, and in my experience, it's a concept that most teachers and writers feel comfortable playing with. In my experience, playfulness perpetuates quality in nearly every context, and my awareness of my audience and my own stance within this work I'm creating has helped me find better words here. I know that many of you are coming from the same place that I do as a writing teacher: Workshop has a long and deep history, and many of us have mastered the terms of its use. I hope to frame things in a way that helps you make connections between what you know and what you're discovering, so that you can plan units and lessons that honor best practices while offering a clear pathway toward what's next.

When writers consider the form that their compositions will take, they explore questions like these:

- What do I want to make?
- What are the smaller parts that make up the whole of this thing?
- What rules do people seem to follow when they make this thing?

Shirel watched several different puppet shows in order to define their common features. She noticed those that were most obvious, and then she began noticing the parts that seemed to make up the whole of each show. There were some rules that she intended to follow as she made her own puppet show. There were a few she planned to break, too. "Because I want it to be funny," she said. "One of my puppets is going to keep popping in and out of the top of the stage, interrupting the main character." She wasn't quite sure what her entire story would be just yet, but thinking through these questions helped her make important decisions about how she would craft it with intention, in order to really engage her audience. It was fascinating to watch this creative process unfold and entirely unlike any approach I'd ever been coached to use as a young writing workshop teacher.

Modes

Each mode of expression offers writers and audiences something that the others cannot. Each combination of modes accomplishes the same. Naming the modes, distinguishing them from one another, and considering their individual and combined potential to influence our audiences in just-right ways is a critical part of the compositional process. It's also what makes this work incredibly creative and complex. Is this sort of decision-making out of reach for very young writers and designers? In my experience, it isn't. I have to plan for it to happen. Often, we make multimodal compositions together—collaboratively—before students create on their own. I also find it important to offer questions like these:

- We could create with letters and words. We could use pictures or drawing. We could build it. We could act it out. We could also make it musical. Which of these choices will help us share our ideas in the very best way? How will we know that we've made a good choice?
- Which of these choices will our audiences like best? Why do we think so?
- Which of these choices are the best fit for the things we are creating? How do we know this?
- What would happen if we tried a different approach?

Puppet shows are quite visual, but aural, spatial, and gestural expression are all at play here, too. I did not use those exact terms with Shirel, but I did invite her to watch another example of a puppet show, challenging her to pay very careful attention to how the puppets and the stage looked, scene by scene. I invited her to pay attention to what she heard—how the puppets were voiced. I also pointed out interesting ways in which the puppets took up space on their stage, how they moved, where, and when.

You may be working with very young writers and designers who are not yet ready to notice all of these things at once. Focusing on the most essential affordances of any single mode may be far more appropriate in these cases. If you're working collaboratively to create a class project, you could assign partners or small groups different things to look for as you explore your own examples together.

Medium and Outlet

Medium refers to the materials and tools that composers use to create a composition. Outlet refers to the place that the work is shared with an audience. The relationship between medium and outlet is so close that it's often difficult to discuss one without referring to the other.

For instance, one writer might use original music and black and white photographs to tell a story on a blog. In this example, music and photography are the media, and the blog is the outlet. Another writer might create comic panels for a newspaper or magazine. Here, the comic panels are the media, and the newspaper or magazine are the outlets.

Sometimes, the medium, or parts of it, is also the outlet. Consider, for instance, a local festival where a composer illustrates a story across a sidewalk using chalk. As children approach, they're invited to add to the story they're viewing. Here, the chalk and the sidewalk are media. They're also outlets. Interestingly enough, the audience members are also the composers.

Writers and designers who have an awareness of their purposes and audiences are better able to choose mediums and outlets where they are most likely to meet them. While you may not expect your students to make such choices independently in kindergarten or first grade, more experienced writers certainly can, especially if they've had the opportunity to share in this kind of decision making during collaborative writing experiences at the primary level. Here are some questions that you might explore together:

- What materials should we use for this project? Why are they good choices?
- Which tools should we use? How will they help us?
- Who is our audience? What kinds of things do these people usually like to read? What do they listen to? Where do they hang out in our community? Where do they spend time online? How do we know?
- What materials and tools should we use to create something wonderful for this audience?
- Where can we share it, so that they'll be sure to see it?

Shirel didn't consider all of these questions of course, but she did sink into one of them. Shirel knew that her puppet show would be performed at our celebration of young writers in the spring. She knew that it would be open to our community and that visitors from outside of our studio would be in the audience watching. "But I want other people to see my puppet show too," she said, once she realized that this was possible. "I wonder where I can share it with people who might like it," she wondered. And this wondering shifted her thinking about medium and outlet. "Maybe I can video record my puppet show on the day of the celebration," she said. "Or maybe, I can make a stop-motion video instead. That might be easier to make and share."

Analyzing Multimodal Mentor Texts

In Chapter 4, I introduced the ACT: The Learning Transfer Mental Model. Conceptualized by Julie Stern, Krista Ferraro, Kayla Duncan, and Trevor Aleo, this model is the perfect vehicle for introducing young writers to the essential elements of multimodal composition before inviting them to design their own (Stern et al., 2021).

Mentor texts play a significant role here. I appreciate the distinctions that Alison Marchetti and Rebekah O'Dell offer in their book, *A Teacher's Guide to Mentor Texts, Grades 6–12* (2021). They tell us that quality mentor texts are engaging, relevant, and professionally crafted guides that inspire writers. They're accessible, and they take many forms (Marchetti & O'Dell, 2021, pp. 4–5).

I'll add that I find that writers are best able to acquire the concepts relevant to the study of most multimodal forms by analyzing mentor texts that are familiar to them before exploring increasingly dissimilar forms. For example, writers might study the concept of story inside of familiar examples composed with written words, such as children's books. These familiar texts are composed with written words, and most young writers are accustomed to encountering stories this way. Next, they might study stories at work inside of a variety of animated shorts before considering the stories conveyed by specific works of art, dance performances, and even musical arrangements.

When we build conceptual understanding by studying genre-specific concepts at work inside of alphabetic or linguistic examples, we remember what we already know. When we connect and then transfer what we've learned about genre through the study of written words to diverse multimodal forms, we widen our aperture for what writing is. We also begin to imagine what it can be.

This is a good place to consider how you might provide the best level of support to the writers and designers you serve. We can differentiate the inquiry and planning process in a way that helps writers of all of them gain solid traction, no matter their age or experience level.

Differentiated Investigations of a Form

Kaya was beginning her third year of teaching when she'd decided that she wanted to bring multimodal composition into her writing workshop. Trained in common workshop practices, she was uncertain how to introduce her second grade students to such wildly diverse forms in a way that would prepare them to produce meaningful work themselves. This is a common kind of dissonance, and I find tools like the one that you see in Figure 6.2 particularly clarifying.

It's best to begin by analyzing examples of the multimodal compositions learners will create, but how do we choose the mentor texts and models that will be studied? More importantly: Who gets to choose them? Whenever

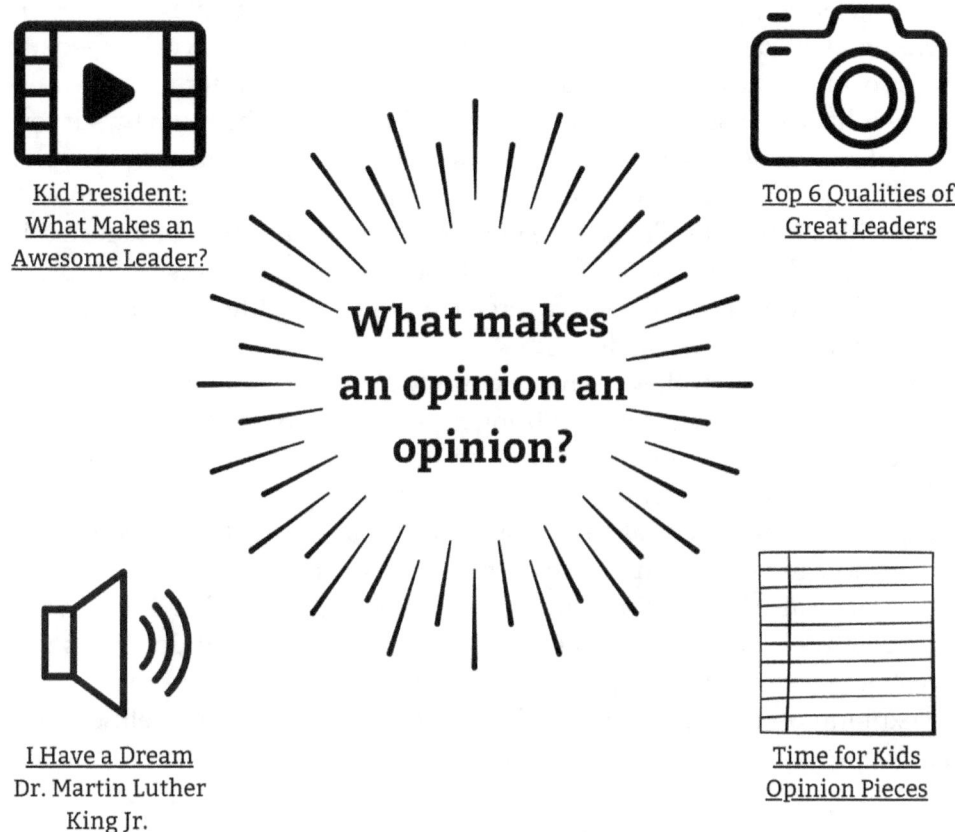

Figure 6.2 Opinions Are Shared Everywhere

I work with teachers of especially young or inexperienced writers, they typically prefer to explore these examples together with their students—as a whole class. And this makes sense. When we're new to something, we often learn better together.

This is why the Gradual Release of Responsibility Model (Fisher & Frey, 2013) has stood the test of time. Mentor texts serve as high quality models of the multimodal compositions we hope to create. After we analyze them, working together to create a collaborative model or prototype lowers the potential for frustration while helping writers and designers build the foundational knowledge and skills they need before we transfer the responsibility for learning and creating to them as independent creators.

But, who gets to decide what everyone will create together during a collaborative multimodal compositional experience? And how should that decision process unfold? Earlier in this chapter, I shared a bit of guidance relevant to defining and getting to know an audience's interests, needs, and preferred outlets. You might begin a collaborative creative experience by deciding as a class which stories, arguments, or facts the world needs to hear most right now. Rather than inviting volunteers to offer ideas by raising their hands, ensure that you hear from everyone in the room by surveying writers and designers, asking each of them to draw or write an idea on a sticky note or index card, or even encouraging them to pitch their proposals along with a rationale. Choose the ideas that most learners are interested in pursuing, and whenever possible, synthesize. If some learners want to create a webpage and others want to create a video, consider building a class webpage that includes a video.

You could take another approach entirely. Rather than investigating mentor texts as a whole class, consider bringing small groups together based upon their interests or their abilities. For example, if some learners want to create videos, others want to create webpages, a third group wants to create comics, and a fourth wants to create a skit, why not situate them by shared interest and encourage them to explore those mentor texts together?

You may also be working with a class with widely varied abilities. In this case, you might decide together which form all writers and designers will investigate and create (puppet shows, for instance). Next, you might invite the exploration of puppet shows that vary by complexity as well. Using a jigsaw approach, learners might meet in homogenous groups first to investigate puppet shows that they might be able to replicate, based upon their unique ability level. Then, serving as a representative of their first group, they might then jigsaw into a new heterogeneous group to share the model they studied, what it taught them about the conventions of puppet shows, and other insights they gained about the form through their investigation of it. This approach exposes learners to a variety of examples.

From there, you might define a more specific audience for your work. And then together, you might explore different multimodal compositions that serve as good mentor texts for the thing that all of you will try to create. This approach is a bit different from what I often see when I visit with teachers in their schools. Too often, it's the adults in the building or worse—vendors—who are choosing what will be created, how, and why. And the only audience for the work is the teacher.

Finally, you may be teaching writers whose experiences and abilities position them as far more independent learners and creators. In this case, the designer's notebook becomes an incredibly powerful tool.

The Designer's Notebook

When students are ready to compose independently, I typically invite them to locate at least three high quality examples of whatever form it is that they intend to create. They use tools much like the one you see in Figure 6.3 to analyze these mentor texts, and they capture their thinking in their notebooks. They also reserve space for reflection and a bit of their own brainstorming. Their notebooks are their own, and while we share peeks into the pages we individually create, I find that writers often arrive at them with their own preferred aesthetic and mental models for organization. I learn a lot by peeking over their shoulders and seeing how they notebook differently than I might.

The notebook is where writers begin sketching up analyses of their chosen mentor texts. Here, they also begin to connect the concepts they acquired, noticing the relationship between different elements and the effect of different choices made by each creator. This prepares them to transfer their understanding of these concepts, how they work individually, and how they influence one another to their own emerging plans.

Those who are creating independently might pitch their ideas to gain valuable feedback from peers, potential audience members, teachers, and those who have expertise with the kind of compositional work they're approaching. You might make space for informal pitching during what would normally serve as an end-of-session writing celebration. You might also create a more elaborate experience that functions much like professional pitch wars do. Spark Tank events, which I referenced in Chapter 5, are an awful lot of fun. I share the gist in Figure 6.4.

Writers acquire knowledge of the essential elements of multimodal composition by identifying them at work inside of examples that are familiar to them. They begin to explore the relationships between these concepts as they connect them to one another inside of increasingly dissimilar examples. Then, they begin to apply this new knowledge to the development of their own project. They gather examples of the form they wish to create, define the conventions of this form, and finally, propose their own project. When writers share these proposals with others, they aim to seek diverse perspectives that can help them improve and innovate upon their work. When writers are invited to consider the pitches offered by their peers, they're often required

THE DESIGNER'S NOTEBOOK

The designer's notebook is a place to analyze the compositions that others create. It's a place to play and plan your own, too.

Audience
- Who is the intended audience, and how do I know?
- What is the author assuming about their identity?
- What values or opinions does this audience hold?
- What design choices did the creator make, in order to serve this particular audience well?
- How is the creator choosing to engage with their audience?

Stance
- What are the creator's intentions?
- What message are they trying to convey?
- What is the creator's primary purpose?
- What other purposes might this work serve?
- What are the unintended consequences of this work?
- How could the creator shift their stance in order to serve their audiences better?

Form
- Which characteristics and features of this form distinguish it from others?
- What conventions do most examples of this form include?
- What do audiences tend to expect when they engage with this particular form?

Modes
- What are the affordances of each mode of expression?
- What makes the creator's choices effective?
- Which modes are most essential to this form?
- How might we tinker with mode and form to discover unexpected and powerful possibilities?

Medium
- What are the affordances of each medium used in this work?
- What is the relationship between the intended audience, media, and outlet?

Use Your Notebook to:

Capture your analyses.

Save clippings of things that inspire you.

Cut things apart and paste them inside, for study or safe-keeping.

Draw the shape of the form you want to create.

Mock something up, create a wireframe, a storyboard, or a mood board.

Keep your ideas.

Experiment with visual elements.

Sketch.

Add QR codes that link to audio or video files.

Dream about what you could make.

Reflect on what you have made.

Use the questions on the left to plan and plan again.

Figure 6.3 The Designer's Notebook

Mentor Texts, Planning, and the Essential Elements of a Multimodal Composition ◆ 103

THE SPARK TANK

WHAT

Inspired by the popular television program that invites entrepreneurs to pitch their ideas to investors who choose whether or not to fund them, a spark tank is a less competitive venture, and no money is involved. Instead, writers and designers pitch working models of their multimodal compositions to classmates and others who offer them meaningful feedback that improves their thinking, process, or work before they over-commit and find themselves experiencing unproductive levels of frustration.

WHEN

Spark tanks are rewarding ways to celebrate the culmination of the planning and prototyping process. Writers and designers pitch imperfect ideas and emerging plans with the intention to spark a bit of inspiration and scoop up new ideas, approaches, and strategies themselves. Rather than making it a competition between students who have created polished products, it's best used as an opportunity to explore ideas that are just taking shape or works in progress.

HOW

- Create a compelling invitation to this special event.
- Workshop how to create a powerful pitch that introduces their idea or work in progress.
- Gather a diverse panel of investors. Include other teachers, staff members, community members, and experts who might offer great insight.
- Invite a surprise guest. Make it someone your students might be interested in learning from outside of your school. Ensure that they have expertise to share.
- If your group is large, consider creating multiple tanks that run at the same time in order to serve all writers and designers well.
- Prepare your investors to offer high quality warm and cool feedback, relevant to the ideas shared, the rhetorical and design choices proposed, and the creative process.
- Plan to document the experience, capturing videos, photographs, observations, and artifacts. Make them widely available to all after the event, so they may workshop with them.

TIPS

Honor the needs and interests of the writers and designers in your room by offering as much choice as possible. Pitches may be audio or video recorded ahead of time so that live performances aren't necessary. They could also be presented on a website, blog, on social media, or inside of an online learning management system. Tools like Flipgrid allow investors to gather remotely and even, asynchronously. Padlet is a powerful option as well. Multimedia spark tanks have many benefits that might make them a preferred option.

Investors who can't be in the room might join remotely, using a video-conferencing tool. Feedback might be offered silently using tools like surveys. You might also structure the event to encourage dialogue and debriefing. This will enable you to assess what is serving everyone well and how to improve the process over time.

Ask your students for their permission to share their pitches with future classes. Models are helpful.

Emphasize and celebrate those moments when new ideas are generated, the creative process is elevated, and writers and designers fail forward.

Figure 6.4 The Spark Tank

to transfer their knowledge of multimodal composition and its essential elements to forms that are quite unlike their own.

This process is one that successfully prepares young writers to prototype multimodal compositions. In fact, it functions like a bit of prototyping before the prototyping, and while it requires a significant time investment, I find that our attention to research, analysis, and the kind of composition that demands the use of written words is time well spent. Writers typically emerge from this phase of the work ready to mock-up a detailed model of their project that enables others to appreciate what the final product might communicate—and how. Depending on their chosen form, they typically work with one of four different kinds of prototyping tools.

How Experienced Writers and Designers Build Prototypes

Graphic organizers might be useful to those composing with written words, but multimodal composition requires different tools that allow plans to function more like prototypes—multidimensional models of what the final form could look like. This kind of complex design work challenges writers to distinguish static from dynamic genres and linear from non-linear texts. This helps them choose just-right planning tools for their projects.

Static texts don't dramatically change when users interact with them, and they don't typically require user interaction in order to function as planned. They include things that young writers and their teachers are accustomed to consuming and creating in a writing workshop or class, such as brochures, flyers, posters, and pre-fabricated charts. They also include uncommon compositional forms such as those products we create with 3-D printers, blueprints, architectural models, and even sculptures. As you might imagine, graphic organizers might be useful planning tools for those creating static texts—especially those that are structured in a linear fashion that invites users to make meaning sequentially.

Dynamic texts often require user interaction to function as planned, largely because how the user engages with the composition changes it in some fundamental way. Examples include websites, social media posts, hyper-docs, video games, digital apps, interactive charts, choose-your-own adventure stories, progressive poems, and tools like Google Maps. Such compositions are often non-linear as well; they flash forward and back, invite swiping, scrolling, or other non-sequential and even layered approaches to navigation. When we consider this, it makes sense that those who create dynamic texts rely on more dynamic planning tools. There are five that tend to serve the writers I support well: storyboards, mood boards, wireframes, scripts, and mock-ups (Arola et al., 2018, pp. 181–197).

Storyboards serve writers who intend to tell a sequential story using a combination of written words, visual elements, and strategic spatial design. Mood boards offer a space for creators to define and then play with color, font, marks, and other aesthetics. Wireframes are useful for web and app design, scripts define who is speaking when and what they're saying inside of a live or recorded performance, and mock-ups are perfect for product prototyping. You'll find examples of each of these at https://angelastockman.com/resources-2/.

Making the Writing Process Multimodal for Inexperienced Writers

While much of this book focuses on how writers and designers create multimodal products, it's incredibly rewarding to invite a multimodal process as well. I've said this often: When we push pencils, pens, and keyboards at writers too soon inside of the process, they will often lower the complexity of their ideas to match their print power. Inviting children to *make* writing helps them scale the barriers created by print. This ensures that their very best ideas and the words that carry them make it to the page.

Here's what that can look like: Once you've defined the elements or pieces of any form, invite writers to use any mode of expression they wish to make or perform those parts. For instance, a writer might use blocks to build a character who faces a problem and then finds a solution inside of a story. Another might use natural elements like leaves, sticks, and stones to build three facts that teach an audience about the Erie Canal. Someone else might doodle a claim and then draw each bit of evidence that supports the claim. When children prototype the whole of what might become a written draft this way, teachers are able to make a quick assessment of their conceptual knowledge as well as their ability to coherently hang their composition together. Once this plan is established, they can begin teaching into that form bit by bit, inviting writers to make just their beginning for instance, and then, use what they've learned from building to transition to written words by labeling, listing, audio recording, and transcribing. Would you like much better guidance here? You'll find the Make Writing Starter Set in the appendix. This is a thick collection of protocols and tools that will help you begin this work in your own writing workshop as soon as tomorrow.

Sixty Second Reflection

In this chapter, we explored the essential elements of a multimodal composition, considered the important role that mentor texts and notebooks might play inside of this work, and then, deepened our planning toolkit by exploring uncommon planning tools and ways in which we might make the process of writing a bit more multimodal. I wonder:

- How might you begin to explicitly teach the essential elements we've examined here?
- How will writers locate and study multimodal mentor texts?
- What role could their notebook play inside of the planning process?
- Which planning tools do they typically use? How might you introduce storyboarding or the use of mood boards, wireframes, scripts, or mock-ups?
- How might you make the writing process a bit more multimodal?
- How is your thinking, learning, or work continuing to change?

References

Arola, K. L., Sheppard, J., & Ball, C. E. (2018). *Writer/designer: A guide to making Multimodal Projects*. Langara College.

Fisher, D., & Frey, N. (2013). *Gradual release of responsibility instructional framework*. Retrieved February 25, 2022, from https://tinyurl.com/mu85f64n

Marchetti, A., & O'Dell, R. (2021). *A teacher's guide to mentor texts: Grade 6–12*. Heinemann.

Stern, J. H., Ferraro, K. F., Duncan, K., Aleo, T., Hattie, J., & Zhao, Y. (2021). *Learning that transfers: Designing curriculum for a changing world*. Corwin.

7

Pitches, Prototypes, and Feedback

Chapter 6 offered perspective on how we might teach multimodal composition, and there, I took a deep dive into the essential elements of multimodal forms and how we might go about helping writers acquire, connect, and then transfer those concepts as they analyze mentor texts or examples before creating drafts or prototypes of their own. What's the difference between these two works in progress? Drafts are usually developed for texts that are composed primarily with written word. Prototypes are a bit similar to the drafts that writers compose with written words in that their purpose, power, and utility are much the same, but they're really preliminary models of multimodal compositions. Let's explore this a bit more.

Multimodal compositions are far more dynamic than texts created with letters and words, and so it makes sense that the initial renderings of these forms are a bit more dynamic. This is why I value planning tools like storyboards, wireframes, mood boards, scripts, and mock-ups. Each offers a structure and a kind of container that helps creators think about how different elements of their form will be represented. When complete, composers share their prototypes with those who are best able to offer critical feedback and inspire further iteration and even innovation. Because prototypes are rapidly produced using cheap materials and few resources, writers are not yet committed to their outcome. Instead, they prototype to bring their initial ideas to life with as much texture and vibrancy as possible. Then, they tinker with them to improve upon those ideas or change them entirely before they invest in the development of the final product.

DOI: 10.4324/9781003216940-11

When it comes time to prototype, I often care less about the aesthetic of the thing and more about the intentions underpinning the design. I care about the degree to which writers have considered the essential elements mentioned in Chapter 6 and the questions aligned to them. I care a great deal about the design choices they're making as well. Here, again, I turned to the work of Kristin L. Arola, Jennifer Sheppard, and Cheryl E. Ball, who speak to the importance of defining and refining these five key concepts: emphasis, contrast, color, organization, alignment, and proximity (Arola et al., 2018, p. 44). There are others of course, and you may choose to identify and use them as well. In my own work with young writers, these are the same design choices that tend to matter most, in most compositional work.

Emphasis

As you read this chapter, you've already encountered the title, a heading, and a narrative citation. Each is placed differently upon this page. They're emphasized so you might notice them. As a writer, I often set words apart, place them in italics or bold, or devote single lines to their expression because it's important to me that you understand their significance. How does emphasis work in a multimodal composition that does not rely heavily on written words? And how might you inspire writers to attend to this facet of design with far greater intention? You might use the ACT Model to design learning experiences that inspire writers to acquire, connect, and then transfer their learning about this concept to their own work.

For example, during the summer of 2021, I brought a multi-age group of writers together for a bit of storymaking fun. The youngest writer in the room was just four years old. The most experienced writer in that same room was 11. Most of these children had spent the better portion of the school year behind them learning online, due to the COVID-19 pandemic.

I introduced the concept of emphasis during a mini-lesson. We studied it inside of a form that was familiar to many of them: SONY Pictures Oscar-winning animated short, *Hair Love* (2019). You can find it yourself through a simple Google search, and I hope that you look for it and watch it. As you do, try to pay attention to what is emphasized and more importantly, *how* the writers and designers relied on modes of expression other than written words to accomplish this. My students zeroed in on two different design choices right away: the use of music and sound effects (aural composition) and facial expression (visual and gestural composition). Even the littlest learners in the room were delighted to make a study of how each character's eyebrows revealed much about their thoughts and feelings, and watching them practice intentional eyebrow design in their own storyboards and Play-Doh creations taught me much about the influence of making not only on writing but on critical thinking and complexity of thought as well.

Next, we studied how mother nature uses emphasis in her designs as well. We took a walk outside, took note of what we saw and heard and felt as a result of her design choices, and gathered natural elements to remake our stories with. Finally, we studied how color could be used to emphasize important elements of a story, using paint chips to prototype our tales. Each shift in perspective and the materials I offered deepened learners' understandings of narrative writing and design concepts. Tinkering with different modes and materials also generated new details and ideas that wouldn't have come to writers through written words alone.

As we studied each mentor text, I prompted writers to look for things that caught their attention. These were design elements that surprised us, helped us understand what was most important, eased our wayfinding, or evoked a strong emotional response. This is how we began to notice what was emphasized in each work, and how.

Picture books may be very different from animated shorts or cartoons, but their creators all rely upon emphasis to connect with, inform, and move their audiences. Emphasis just looks and works differently, depending on the form and the context creators are working within.

The design choices that follow shaped our perspectives further. I find that teaching them one at a time matters. This is complex learning and complicated work. When I introduce each concept of an experience intended to help writers acquire knowledge of each concept before connecting it to mentor texts, noticing relationships between this and other concepts, and then, transferring their understandings to uncommon forms and their own compositions, their process is productive. When I don't take care to coach concept acquisition before connection and connection before transfer, thinking is quickly muddied and frustration follows.

I'm also thoughtful about how many of these concepts we study at once or even over the course of time as a lengthier learning experience unfolds. When I'm working with very young writers, we might study emphasis throughout an entire unit rather than sprinkling in shallower studies of those concepts that follow. Consider the form that writers are creating, the examples you're sharing, and which design choices might be most obvious to your students. These are perfect entry points into the explicit instruction of multimodal composition.

Contrast

Contrast is often what makes emphasis possible. When a writer creates contrast in a written work, they juxtapose one element of the form against another. For instance, I might emphasize the headings in this book by placing them on their own lines, altering the font size or type, and perhaps, using bold print. This contrast sets my headings apart from my paragraphs, and this helps my readers identify what's essential and how information is organized, so that they may find their way through the text and comprehend it with ease. As Arola, Sheppard, and Ball explain, color, size, placement, shape, and content influence the way we approach contrast in any text. The elements that we choose to contrast are those that are most emphasized to our audiences (Arola et al., 2018, p. 45).

Writers might acquire knowledge of these concepts by identifying each of them at work inside of multimodal forms that they're quite familiar with: favorite photos, videos, websites, and children's books and illustrations. More experienced writers and designers might even begin to notice the relationship between them—how one influences another—as they explore the design choices made by the creators of unfamiliar works. Once writers have acquired and begun connecting these concepts, they will be better prepared to attend to them in their own work.

For instance, the creators of *Hair Love* (2019) use contrasting sound effects to reveal shifts in each character's experience or emotions. Notice how the music changes when characters are happy, when they're sad, when they're frustrated, or when surprising things happen. These are complex design choices that even very young learners can typically appreciate.

Color

Composers use color to create contrast and emphasis. It's used for juxtapositional purposes inside of visual texts. Consider the way black elements appear against a white backdrop, for instance. Consider how white elements appear when placed upon a black background instead. Color has an emotional effect on audiences, and artists of all kinds leverage this with intention. Writers will pen lines about a character's blue, melancholy mood. Photographers create steely settings by capturing gray skies in just-right light. Color carries cultural meaning as well. For instance, in Native American cultures, orange is often associated with learning and kinship, while other cultures associate it primarily with Halloween.

Inviting writers to identify the design choices that other creators have made relevant to color is an important first step in using it in their own work. Most writers have some awareness of how color is used to reflect or create mood and other meaning in multimodal texts. Spending some time exploring different cultural interpretations is powerful here as well. Uncovering these subtle craft moves adds richness and complexity to the analysis of any work. It also inspires writers to be thoughtful about color as they approach their own.

I'm reminded of the designers who created Disney Pixar's charming film, *Inside Out* (2015). Color is used with great intention to portray the characters of Sadness (who is blue), Joy (who is yellow), Disgust (who is green), Fear (who is purple), and Anger (who is red). Can you think of forms that use color with clear intention? Share all of them beside one another as you explore this design move with students. It's helpful for them to notice it at work inside of very different examples.

Organization

Anyone who has recently stepped into a department store they've frequented for years only to find its floor plan completely redesigned appreciates the influence of organization inside of design. Organization refers to the way in which the parts of a composition hang together to form a meaningful whole. In my experience, organization tends to be valued least by those designers who maintain a preference for form over function. Many inexperienced writers and designers seem to fall into this category and so, I often find myself posing clarifying questions that intend to inspire careful thought here.

For instance, an aesthetically pleasing website is of no value to a user if they're unable to navigate it with ease. When we fail to plot a narrative well, we often lose readers along the way. And when listeners tune in to a podcast unable to determine who is speaking and why, they'll typically tune out moments later. Other design choices might help us hook our audience, but the way a piece is organized sustains their engagement. When multimodal compositions are incoherent or impossible to use, people tend to walk away. Incoherence is common in the work of emerging writers and designers, and this provides ample opportunity for instruction.

Facilitating learning opportunities that deepen students' organizational skills are very different from imposing organizational frames on writers and their work. When we give writers graphic organizers that define *the* structure of a piece, we miss the opportunity to coach critical thinking and creativity. When we analyze examples of the compositions we hope to replicate, tease out their defining elements or parts, and then, tinker around with their order and consider how different organizational relationships change and even improve the work, we encourage innovation.

Here's how this recently looked inside of an elementary writing workshop where I was invited to facilitate a lesson study for teachers: Writers who were interested in designed web pages analyzed several examples with me in order to define their working parts. Each writer sketched these essential elements, and then, they used scissors to cut them out. As they planned their own web pages, they played around with organization a bit, tinkering with layout, and seeking feedback from others on their new designs. Studying mentor texts helped them define what was important and how some website designers chose to organize their compositions. Sketching the organizational structure helped them visualize one way to create their own—these sketches served as graphic organizers of sorts. Cutting them apart and experimenting with organizational options inspired them to see what could be, or what was, possible while maintaining quality and coherence.

Alignment

Alignment refers to the way we line elements up inside of a text. Those who work with written words understand center, right, and left justification. We spend much time helping emerging readers and writers compose and consume written words from left to right. Quality composers in every field design their work in ways that are at the very least useful and efficient and at best, downright delightful. While it's easy to consider alignment in the context of written words, it plays an important role in all multimodal design.

In my experience, inviting writers to identify alignment inside of compositions that rely on visual and spatial expression is an especially clarifying first step. We might study infographics, magazine layouts, posters, or photographs. It's fun to consider alignment by watching marching bands perform or dance troupes. It's easy to notice its influence at work inside of compositions like these. Here's something else: I find that when I'm able to share contrasting views of alignment inside of multiple and varying models, writers develop a crisper acquisition of this concept.

Proximity

When we make a study of proximity, we pay attention to the placement of elements in relationship to one another. This is different from noticing how elements are aligned. Proximity challenges us to understand that closeness and distance affect message and meaning.

Considering Design Choices in Mentor Texts

As writers explore examples of the kind of compositions they hope to create, the language of the essential elements introduced in Chapter 6 and their attention to the design choices introduced here sharpens their vision and enables them to define the conventions of their own chosen form. This looks different in middle and high school classrooms than it might in kindergarten, third, or fifth grade.

For instance, when I'm supporting older and more experienced writers, we will often analyze multiple essential elements and multiple design choices within the same learning experience. These are concepts that I will eventually expect these young writers and designers to evaluate independently and then, transfer to their own work. When I'm supporting much younger and less experienced writers, we will often look for the presence of just one essential element inside of multiple mentor texts. We might consider just one kind of design choice that a creator made inside of a complex composition. I rely on formative assessment heavily here, paying attention to how quickly and deeply learners are mastering and transferring concepts to their own creations before illuminating others and inviting additional analysis and application to their own creative work.

I'm still learning here myself, and your experiences and mileage may vary. In short, I'm finding that the more intentional I am about naming, helping writers and designers acquire and then transfer these concepts to their own compositions, the more intentional they are about the choices they are making. They offer meaningful rationales, and the quality of what they produce is more sophisticated.

Learning more about how to talk with writers and designers has been critical to my own growth as a writing teacher who is welcoming multimodal composition into her workshop. Language matters because it helps us understand and support one another better as we bring these new and very dynamic forms into our writing community. Explicit instruction matters because it helps writers acquire, connect, and transfer these new concepts to their own work. When it comes to creating a community where multimodal composition is welcome, I find that something else matters quite a bit—the collective intelligence of every writer and designer in the room, and making space for everyone to share and benefit from it. Pitching ideas in order to invite peer review is one great way to accomplish this.

Pitching to Peer Review

When I suggest that even kindergarteners can pitch their plans and engage in high quality peer review, many teachers are initially skeptical. This might be why this is one of my favorite things to demonstrate in my Make Writing Studio sessions. Here's how it typically looks:

- Writers and designers create a storyboard, a vision board, a wireframe, or a mock-up of the composition they wish to create.
- They use this plan to pitch their idea to other writers in the room, live or via video recording.
- Other writers in the room offer warm and cool feedback (rather than compliments or criticism).
- Writers and designers decide what of that feedback, if anything, they will use to change their plan.

Consider the protocol in Figure 7.1. How might you invite your students to use it as they write and design and support other writers and designers? I've been relying on some form of this approach for well over a decade now, after Dr. Giselle Martin-Kniep, Joanne Picone-Zocchia, and Diane Cunningham introduced it to me at a Communities for Learning: Leading Lasting Change summer retreat (Martin-Kniep et al., 2008). Experience has taught me that acclimating writers and designers to this protocol is not the work of a single lesson or even a week or an entire school year. Becoming a skilled feedback provider requires abundant, consistent practice. That practice can begin in kindergarten. Although this particular framing might work better for more sophisticated writers, you'll find additional tools in the Talking with Writers (and Designers!) document available at https://angelastockman.com/resources-2/.

As a teacher, I find that formative assessment is an important part of this process. I introduce the concept of warm feedback first, offer examples and frames, and then make time for practice. I document what I'm noticing. This informs my next bit of instruction. My hope is that by mid-course, writers and designers will be able to engage in high quality peer review and offer one another solid feedback with far less intervention on my behalf. This is slow and steady work, and I must manage my expectations, especially early on. Writers will not be particularly good at this. That doesn't mean I will stop inviting them to try, noticing where I might serve them better, and offering them just-right guidance.

Here's something else that you might appreciate: While it's important that writers ask for and provide high quality feedback to one another, I've found

A PEER REVIEW PROTOCOL

The Protocol:

As each prototype is pitched, document specific observations about the rhetorical and design choices made.

When the pitch is over, ask any clarifying questions that require answers so that you fully understand the creator's intentions and work.

Pause to quietly compose both warm and cool feedback, referring specifically to things you saw and heard.

Offer just one bit of warm feedback first, and wait for other reviewers to follow your contribution with one bit of warm feedback each. Then, offer another bit and wait for other reviewers to do the same. Continue in these rounds until all warm feedback has been shared.

Then, offer cool feedback one bit at a time, in rounds.

If your work is under review, document the feedback you receive so that you may evaluate its usefulness and determine if and how you will use it.

Warm Feedback	Cool Feedback
<ul><li>Illuminates where the writer is meeting goals.</li><li>References specific design or rhetorical moves and the conventions of the genre.</li><li>Reveals a level of attention to the work that requires elaboration, moving beyond simple compliments.</li></ul>	<ul><li>Demonstrates where the writer is ready to pursue goals.</li><li>Prompts reflection through questioning rather than correction through direction.</li><li>Reveals a level of attention to the work that reflects an interest in the creator's success, moving beyond simple criticism.</li></ul>

Figure 7.1 A Peer Review Protocol

it's incredibly rewarding for them to seek out members of their intended audiences. When writers and designers pitch ideas to them, the feedback they receive is often quite different than what their classmates provide. It's even more motivating. These exchanges seem to legitimize the process, moving it into the realm of "real world" writing far ahead of any official launch. This is another way we assure writers that it's the process and not only the product that counts.

I find that authentic pitches and proposals—the kind that we encounter every day in our schools and organizations—make for meaningful and manageable design work and higher quality peer review. Again, ensuring that the models we share are ones that students recognize and have the ability to replicate is important. Proposals are made on a daily basis inside of so many learning and professional communities. As an instructional designer, I find myself pitching ideas, asking for feedback, and tinkering with my own prototypes at least a few times a week, if not more. It's likely that you do, too. Why not document this? Why not share these experiences—and those of other human beings in our orbit—regularly with young writers and designers? When they begin to see all of the different ways people of all ages make and pitch their ideas—from complex projects to simple solutions—they'll be better prepared and far more confident about doing it themselves.

I'm thinking of my colleagues Peter Schilke and Eric Hill at Daemen College in Amherst, New York. When our campus launched a door decorating contest for homecoming week, they began pitching ideas for the theme and design of our office door. Their initial proposals were loose, even a bit incoherent. But the more they shared, and the more feedback they received, the more coherent and feasible their ideas became. In the end, our final plan was a synthesis of several, and our mock-up of this model guided our actual design, which incorporated every mode of composition with the exception of aural and haptic expression.

I'm also reminded of my daughter Laura. She's a Brooklyn-based designer who creates branding packages for individuals and agencies of all kinds. She begins her projects by assessing the needs, interests, and vision of the clients that she serves, and then she creates mood boards that reveal potential color, font, texture, layout, and illustration choices. She designs these rapidly and then, seeks early and consistent feedback from her clients before over committing to the actual work. Pitches and prototypes like these sustain her energy and prevent her from wasting time and resources. These same benefits serve very young designers and their teachers as well.

I'm wondering what your own experiences with prototyping and pitching have been. I'm wondering how you might document your future experiences with each. Doing so would provide you with the artifacts you need to bring these processes to life in a way that is meaningful and manageable for your students. Inviting them to do the same would help you curate a growing collection of student-created examples.

The questions that follow offer an opportunity to reflect and connect them to the learning we've done in this chapter. Doing so might help you identify entry points for your students as they approach similar work.

Sixty Second Reflection

Quality pitches typically lead to the creation of successful prototypes. Whether we're aware of it or not, people are pitching us almost daily. My daughter Nina pitched a bedroom redesign shortly after dinner this evening. Tomorrow, I plan to pitch a proposal to my program director about hosting an EdCamp on our campus. My daughter's purposes and plans are very different from my own, but both of us benefited from sharing our ideas and seeking feedback before investing a lot of time, energy, and resources in our work. I wonder:

- When was the last time you were pitched on a new concept, idea, or product? What do you recall about the creator's idea and the feedback offered? Use what you learned in the last two chapters to help you reflect, if you need to.
- When was the last time you pitched a concept, idea, or product of your own? Why did you do this? What was the result?
- How might you help the writers you serve plan and then pitch their own ideas for the multimodal compositions they might create?
- How might you facilitate the feedback process?
- How has your thinking changed after reading this chapter?

References

Arola, K. L., Sheppard, J., & Ball, C. E. (2018). *Writer/designer: A guide to making Multimodal Projects*. Langara College.

Disney Pixar. (2015). *Inside Out*. Retrieved from https://movies.disney.com/inside-out.

Martin-Kniep, G., Picone-Zocchia, J., & Cunningham, D. (2008). Communities for learning: Leading lasting change summer retreat. West Cornwall, CT.

SONY Pictures Animation. (2019). *Hair Love*. Retrieved February 25, 2022, from https://youtu.be/kNw8V_Fkw28.

Stern, J. H., Ferraro, K. F., Duncan, K., Aleo, T., Hattie, J., & Zhao, Y. (2021). *Learning that transfers: Designing curriculum for a changing world*. Corwin.

8

Launching a Multimodal Composition into the World

Sometimes, I wonder if we talk about publishing in ways that are less than helpful to the young writers and designers we serve. I know that when I think about publishing, I tend to imagine powerful people in powerful places deciding whose voices and work will be shared with the world and whose will not. I envision towering piles of proposals and manuscript submissions that will never make the cut. I remember the school counselor I approached at the start of seventh grade when I was eager to submit my writing to a real market. She wasn't certain that any existed for children, she admitted. And if there were such markets, it would be very unlikely that my work would be chosen. And anyway, I was failing Algebra. Shouldn't I be focused on that instead?

When I was young, published writers were much like unicorns: magical. Mythical. This isn't true anymore.

Here's a bit of serendipity. As I'm typing these lines, the morning news is introducing me to Dillon Helbig, an 8 year-old writer from Boise, Idaho, who was so eager to see his own book on a library shelf that he put it there himself, when the librarians were not looking (Fadel, 2022). And when they happened upon it, they made it an official library book, and now, an impressive list of readers are wait-listed and eager to borrow it.

My own daughter Laura started a blog when she was ten years old and found herself an audience overnight. Nearly 15 years ago, middle school writers in my studio self-published their own novels. My friend Sandy has built a rewarding writerly life for herself doing much the same.

And the internet changes everything.

Opportunity abounds for writers and designers who are ready to launch their work into the world. They don't need anyone's permission, unless they're specifically seeking it. Publishing is a post, a Tweet, or an update away. This is exciting. It's also daunting, and our responsibilities are greater than ever here.

If you follow the instructional approaches I recommend in Chapters 6 and 7, then the writers you support may be defining and engaging with their potential audiences long before they put the finishing touches on their multimodal compositions. They'll actually create and evolve their work with their audiences in mind and their input to guide them. Each movement they make from the inception of their idea to the launch of their final product provides opportunities for writers to learn more about how well their efforts might serve the people they're speaking to. This is as true for five-year-olds as it is for 10- or 11- or 12-year-olds. Their purposes and products may be very different, and the people they engage as audience members may be, too. In general though, most young writers are moved to create things because their audiences are people they're already connected to and they're eager to move them in some way.

By the time their work is complete, many young writers have likely given good thought to how they might launch their work into the world, which outlets might help them reach their audiences best, and when might be the perfect moment to make the big reveal. This chapter offers some final guidance and a few approaches that serve to deepen and perhaps, even push your perspectives a bit before final decisions are made. Let's begin by exploring how very young and inexperienced writers might share their multimodal compositions with audiences who truly appreciate them. Then, we'll consider different ways to help experienced writers bring their work into the world.

Helping Our Youngest Writers Create Things for Authentic Purposes

I've always been a bit bothered by the way we bat around the concept of "authentic audience" in the field. Typically, it shows up whenever someone like me, an author or consultant, wants to point out how different schoolified curriculum, instruction, and assessment might be from what we see in the "real" world. In my opinion, school is a very real world, and writers do find audiences there. Nothing is imaginary. It's all authentic. It's not always meaningful, though.

Even our youngest and least experienced writers enjoy producing purposeful things. They may not yet be seeking agents, publishers, or markets in the way that more sophisticated writers do, but they absolutely love connection—as all humans do. And when their work connects with people who are authentically delighted, informed, called to action, or otherwise moved, they begin to understand the power of publication. They begin to create for increasingly meaningful purposes.

How might you invite five-, six-, seven-, and eight-year-olds to make things that truly move people? Here are ten different ideas for you, and I've linked to resources, tools, and examples in the appendix:

- Design a class newspaper, magazine, newsletter, or anthology using Google Docs or Canva so that it's easy to use multimedia to capture the best of multimodal work. Create a quick installation of student work by inviting writers and designers to leave their finished products on their desks, along with artist's statements. Invite classmates, families, friends, and other school community members to tour the room, meet the writers and designers, and celebrate their learning and work.
- Consider audio recording each artist's statement, along with other reflections on their thinking, learning, and work. Make a playlist, and provide it to installation visitors so that they may listen to it on a self-guided tour.
- Move the installation to the library, and situate compositions within the shelves that house books that are most relevant to each work.
- Create a little free library of student created books that can be signed out. Consider using copies rather than the originals, so that as things are inevitably lost, they are easy to replace.
- Build a little free library for your school's front lawn, and fill it with student work.
- Compose collaborative arguments that might inspire necessary change in your school or community. Invite each learner to speak just one small piece of the whole, and audio or video record it. Share this synthesis of student voices with the leaders who most need to hear it.
- Leverage your social media network to partner with another teacher and class from a different state or country. Publish works for one another, and celebrate your shared learning.
- Take a walking field trip around the community, take photos of things you're collectively grateful for, and make a thankful book. Share it with the people who created or maintain those spaces.
- Identify an unsung hero in your community, make something wonderful that recognizes them, and work together to design and deliver it well.

- Create stop motion videos, shadow puppet theaters, or tiny box projects that communicate meaningful messages. Publish them on YouTube, your school website, or in a classroom blog or newsletter. Leverage Twitter to create a more global audience for this work. Or come find me there. I'll happily share within my wider network.
- Install multimodal compositions in widely accessible places within your school—on the walls in the halls, in showcases, in libraries and cafeterias, and on digital monitors and screens. Consider using images of student work as screensavers on shared devices. Ask your building principal to mention a few students' pieces each day on the morning announcement, and make sure every student's work is recognized by year's end.
- And of course, you can use any number of apps, tools, and devices to create ebooks, portfolios, websites, blogs, podcasts, and other multimedia publications. You might work on these collaboratively, as an entire class or in small groups. Students might create things independently as well. I've shared some of my favorite tools in the appendix. All of them are easy enough for primary level writers to create with on their own. Look for the Multimodal Mentor Texts and Tools there.

Helping More Experienced Writers and Designers Launch Their Work

While very young and inexperienced writers and designers often create for audiences that are defined, to a significant degree, by their teachers, our efforts to support students' pursuit of publication evolve quite a bit as they gain more confidence in their abilities to make their own decisions.

Rather than carving distinct pathways, we might find ourselves offering increasingly complex maps, guiding their wayfinding, and then watching them navigate the road and eventually the globe independently. What does that even look like? Where do learners begin?

There are several points to ponder here.

Of course, writers will want to consider where their audiences tend to be most present—physically and virtually. They'll want to consider which of those spaces are most appropriate for them to share their work within. Then, they'll need to consider when and how they might accomplish this. Choosing the best outlet also requires creators and the teachers who support them to consider issues of privacy, online safety, and etiquette. These questions are worth considering, and the answers that you uncover together will help writers make wise choices.

- Which outlets have longevity? It makes sense to consider sharing work inside of spaces that are well-established and have a greater likelihood of remaining online over time.
- Which outlets actively protect creators and their work? Are privacy and accessibility statements visible? Do writers agree with those terms? Are you comfortable with them, too? What are the community guidelines, and who is responsible for upholding them? How open is this space, and what is done to ensure that users are able to engage there safely? Finally, what will students risk in terms of their own rights to their work by sharing it within a chosen space? It might be helpful to conduct a quick search to get a sense of each outlet's reputation among other teachers. Place the name of the outlet inside of quotation marks, add the words "and problematic" or "and reputation" or "and complaints" and see what your efforts return. If you have a professional learning network, invite their perspective, too. Feel free to tweet at me if you'd like a signal boost. I'm glad to help.
- Which school policies must you honor as you support writers through the publication process? Which ones do harm, and how might you challenge them? Investigate this and align your decision-making accordingly.
- To what degree should a child's guardians be involved in this decision making process? Be sure to reach out to your building or district leaders for guidance here before launching student work.
- What can students do to protect their rights to their work before they go public? Consider Creative Commons and copyright protections.
- Finally, how do people engage within the spaces that students intend to publish within? What are the rules of acceptable use, and how is netiquette practiced there? What do all of you notice about this, and how might it inform your choices and your behavior, should you choose to enter the space?

Timing the Launch

Much of what we've explored in this text has everything to do with the meaningfulness of a writer's work. Relevance matters as well. When writers have the opportunity to launch a just-right project at a just-right time, they're far more likely to influence their audiences in the ways that they imagined. Much of our thinking about the context of any work, the intended audience, their interests, and their needs informs the decisions that writers may make about when they will send their work out into the world. Questions like these are useful:

- How are current events shaping my audience's opinions, interests, and needs? How might my work accomplish the same? How might I time its release with intention, in order to achieve what I hope to?
- Is there a perfect time of year or season to share my work within?
- Is my audience more engaged at certain times of the day?
- Where does my audience live? How does this influence their time zone, and how does their time zone compare to my own? What implications should I be aware of here?

Considering the unintended consequences of publishing, presenting, and performing writers—even experienced, adult writers—are often idealistic about the pursuit of publication. Many imagine that their work will be consumed by a wide audience. Some assume that it will be deeply appreciated as well. This leads to disappointment when creators learn that only a few people have taken the time to explore what they've shared and even fewer have expressed any real interest in it. Those that are seeking validation might struggle when their audiences question, challenge, or criticize what they've created. Those seeking meaningful feedback are often just as disappointed when audiences offer applause and nothing more.

Defining our expectations, learning how to manage them, and considering the unintended consequences of publishing our work is an important part of the process, but I know few writing teachers, including myself, who invest significant time here.

We rarely challenge writers to consider the sustainability of their work, either. I remember when my daughter was ten and just learning to blog, refusing her requests to start new sites until she had taken the time to frame up a pretty solid proposal for her work. Students need to consider what's worthy of publication, what is not, and when it makes sense to keep works in process in draft form, rather than sharing things that are not yet reflective of their best work. Just as young professionals need to take care to manage their social media presence so as not to undermine their potential to secure decent jobs, so too do young writers who share unfinished, unpolished examples of their own work in spaces that are difficult to sustain over time.

It's common for young writers to believe that once they ship a project, their engagement with it ends. This isn't the case in the digital world, where audiences continue to access, use, and comment on content that is still available many years after it was initially posted. Inviting writers to create a long-term

PREPARING TO LAUNCH

The questions below help writers and designers define and make good choices as they prepare to launch their work into the world. It's useful to share them at the beginning of a new genre study as learners are studying the work of other creators and beginning to define their own purposes and audiences as well.

Spaces and Places

Where does the intended audience spend time?

Which face-to-face or virtual spaces invite this type of work for this type of audience?

Which publications might be promising?

Media and Mode

Which media best engage the intended audience?

Which modes of expression best communicate the intended message?

Which spaces and places make room for these types of work?

Timing

When is the best time to launch, and how does the creator know?

What's happening in the world? How might this inform the timing of the launch?

How might time of day and time-zone differences inform planning?

Netiquette and Etiquette

How are people expected to behave in these spaces?

How are these expectations shared?

How are they managed?

How do these values align with the creator's?

School Policies

Which policies must be considered?

What are the purposes of such policies?

Who is protected by the policy?

How might we challenge policies that do harm?

Privacy and Rights

How is privacy protected?

How are spaces moderated?

How are the creator's rights to the work protected or put at risk?

What might the creator do to protect privacy and rights ahead of launch?

Figure 8.1 Preparing to Launch

management plan is a useful endeavor that ensures that writers are sharing and updating their very best work so that it continues to reflect the very best of who they are creatively. When such planning doesn't seem productive or feasible, it makes sense to define when the work will be removed from the web and who will be responsible for removing it.

Reflecting to Learn

Finally, it makes good sense for writers to consider publication a significant part of the learning process that can help them better their work. After all, it's often once the work has been launched into the world that audiences begin to react to it. This feedback can inform refinements and entire revisions, and the nature of today's publishing tools and apps helps writers accomplish this efficiently.

Sometimes, the feedback that writers receive has less to do with the form of the work and how expertly the writer crafted their message and more to do with the implications of sharing that message within a certain context, including those they aren't familiar with. Some audience members are brave enough to challenge those who publish things that push their thinking or more importantly, hurt them or those they care about. Preparing learners to respond well is an important part of this work.

Earlier, we considered the influence of context on meaning, and it's important to note here that even when we make an effort to deepen students' cultural intelligence, it's impossible for anyone to know what they don't know. Harm may still be done, criticisms may be raised, and—legitimate or not—today's writers need to be aware of this reality and know how to respond responsibly.

When young writers and designers are explicitly taught that their creative context may not be the one that their audiences bring to the work, they can explore the potential ramifications and prepare to address them sensitively.

It's important for writers and designers to know that while it may not be anyone's intention to create something hurtful, the fact is that many of us do, and when we're made aware of this, we need to take responsibility for the harm done and make efforts to repair it.

This isn't about inspiring guilt or fear. It's about ensuring that the writing workshops and communities we create prepare all participants for these realities, because all writers and designers experience them. Responsible writers and designers take care to handle themselves ethically and empathetically inside of them. This calls us to deepen our self-awareness, examine power dynamics and imbalances, and know our place inside of certain contexts.

Preparing students for this potential and teaching them how to proceed in ways that intend to heal any hurt is crucial. When we fail to do this, we run the risk of putting young writers and designers in situations that they did not anticipate and that they are also ill-equipped to handle well. Preparing them well ensures that the creative process is one that grows them as humans. Ultimately, that is one of the greater rewards of launching our work. Learning how to meet other humans honestly, respectfully, and humbly is a beautiful byproduct of publishing, presenting, or performing. It isn't always comfortable, but great learning often isn't.

Many find this framing helpful, and I encourage young people to use it when they're made aware that they've offended someone or more importantly, injured them with their work or their actions: "I apologize. My intention was x, and I didn't realize that my choices caused y. I will do z in order to fix this." It's that simple, and it's also that hard. Offering this inside of a lesson that serves an entire workshop ahead of any turbulence is typically far more meaningful than using it as an intervention when one writer or designer's behavior or work is challenged. All of us may be challenged at one point or another. All of us need to know how to respond in ways that make that moment one that deepens learning, opportunities for reparation, and restoration.

Publication Outlets for Writers of All Ages

There are a number of reliable places where even very young writers are welcome to share their work. Some accept and publish a limited number of submissions. Others are less discriminating, and there is a wide variety of outlets where anyone who chooses to share their work may do so without anyone's approval. Once writers have considered the questions I shared earlier in this chapter, some might begin to peruse the options available in the appendix. This is a collection that I update regularly, and you may return to it over time to access the most recent updates. If you have recommendations, please reach out to let me know. I'd love to add them.

Sixty Second Reflection

Publication serves writers as well as their audiences—in different ways and to different degrees. As you begin to consider how you will approach this work in your own classroom, I wonder:

- What excites you about inviting authentic publication? What do you want to try?
- What gives you pause as you consider inviting authentic publication? How might you plan to ensure that all goes well?

- How might you invite your students to approach publication as the start of the revision or iterative process?
- How has your thinking, learning, or work continued to change?

Reference

Fadel, L. (2022). Eight-year-old Idaho boy hides his self-made book on library's shelf [Radio broadcast]. NPR. https://www.npr.org/transcripts/1077522564

Appendix A

Planning Tools

Andrea Schaber's Story

How has multimodal composition supported our youngest learners?

Being a kindergarten teacher at the beginning of a new school year is filled with so much adorable chaos. I've heard people refer to the process as herding kittens, and to be honest, it's a pretty accurate description. One second students are bouncing around giggling over conversations about seemingly random topics like maple syrup on bananas, the next they are crying and stomping over broken blue crayons, after that, they are engaging in wildly mature conversations regarding ways to save our planet, and then, they are falling asleep face first on a pile of math manipulatives. Learning new academic and social routines can certainly be exhausting, for kids and adults alike! These tiny humans are bursting with different emotions every other minute. Someone is missing their grownups at home, someone is telling a story about their mom's brother's house with the pink door and dog named George, someone loves your new haircut, someone likes your hair the "old way," someone is reminding you about their playdate this afternoon and going on bus #5 instead of bus #2, and someone is quietly coloring a picture at the blue table to glue onto the wall in the back of the classroom, because, "that wall was just too plain." Even in the midst of so much excitement and unpredictability, one thing remains certain: nothing beats the magic of building a classroom community with a group of eager four- and five-year-olds who are curious to explore the world around them. I really don't know of many greater privileges than to be a part of this heart-warming, head spinning, and humbling learning experience.

So how does this range of energy and emotion relate to writing workshop and multimodal composition? How do these characteristics transfer to identity affirming and equitable teaching practices and learning experiences? How can we, as educators, possibly meet the vast variety and ever changing personalities and learning styles of every child throughout the school day? For a while, I thought these answers could be found in a structured, organized, workshop model during the literacy block in my classroom. And while I wasn't entirely right about this, I wasn't entirely wrong, either.

Early in my teaching career when I would begin introducing reading and writing workshop to my kindergarteners, I would commonly hear, "but I don't know how to read!" and "I don't know how to write!" My responses to these worries changed over the years, mostly based on my experiences and the definitions I've assigned to the words, "reading" and "writing," but also due to some critical mindset and instructional shifts. Nonetheless, I would introduce my students to the workshop model, but no matter how tightly I scaffolded the process, I would still be met with a handful of students demonstrating feelings of anxiety and frustration. Students needing constant reassurance, crumpled up papers, scribbling over work, avoidant behaviors and frequent trips to the bathroom, negative self-talk, and the list goes on and on. I created opportunities for conferencing, partner work, targeted small group instruction, and as many visuals and toolkits I could find. I was missing something here, and felt like I was letting my students down. How could I address the unique learning styles of every child in my classroom during reading and writing workshop?

Angela Stockman was hosting a Make Writing Workshop with a group of elementary aged students in our district one summer, and I was in the small group of educators who had the incredible privilege of observing these sessions and debriefing our learning with Angela after each lesson. To say this experience was rewarding would be an extreme understatement. Watching Angela model for and guide the students through this Make Writing Workshop process, while allowing students to take the lead on demonstrating their own thinking and learning through multimodal experiences, was nothing short of remarkable. Angela quickly gathered information from the students about their unique experiences and stories with firestarter prompts, supplied students with a wide array of resources and materials, and created scaffolded supports for students to build, create, and even share their beautiful stories. It was this truly fluid process where students immediately found their own voices through various modes of expression, and shared their stories bravely and freely. The students were seamlessly self-assessing, peer-assessing, seeking feedback, reflecting, and revising their own pieces as the sessions progressed. Through this multimodal process, every child's beautiful voice was seen, heard, and honored. Within this completely reimagined workshop model, being a "writer" held an entirely new meaning.

I couldn't let these incredible multimodal Make Writing experiences pass me by, nor could the other educators in the room. We created a learning team and planned to meet with Angela several times throughout the upcoming school year. We created entry points in our upcoming writing workshop units to incorporate these multimodal opportunities for our students. The benefits of these experiences went far beyond the walls of the writing workshop; they changed the way I learned about my students as learners, the way my students learned about themselves as learners, and the way I planned for and designed learning experiences for every lesson and unit moving forward. This multimodal mindset shift in writing workshop was one of the most eye-opening experiences in my career as an educator. This mindset has inspired my beliefs in working to foster identity affirming spaces, environments where students are consistently met with learner centered experiences, and equitable opportunities to demonstrate thinking and learning through various modes of expression.

Offering students a wide range of materials during writing workshop helps support their planning and building process and leads to more elaboration and detailed storytelling.

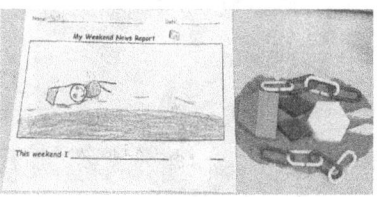

 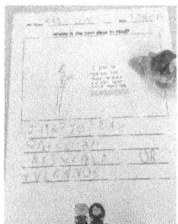   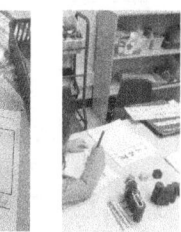

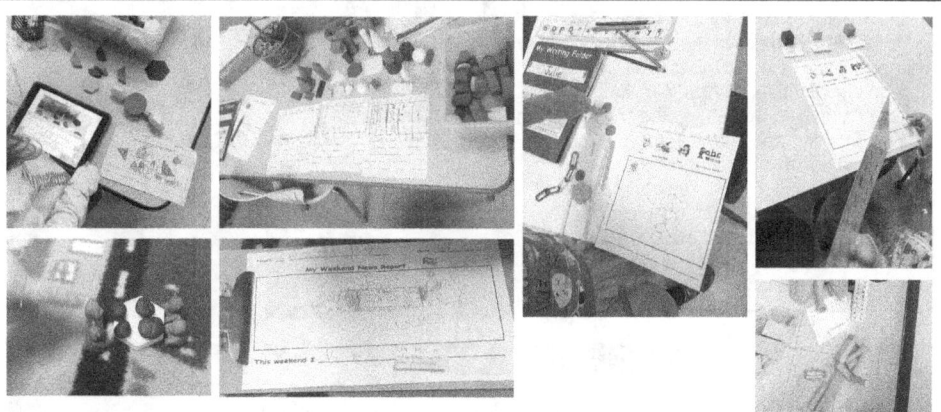

Students are able to transfer their building and planning to paper, while continuing to use other tools to support their writing process. Students begin to find their voice in the way they sequence the events of their stories which supports them as they transfer to print. Encouraging students to take pictures and audio record supports their progression over time as they build on their previous day's work. This is also helpful as the teacher when reviewing student work to plan for next steps.

Copyright material from Stockman (2023), *The Writing Workshop Teacher's Guide to Multimodal Composition (K–5)*, Routledge.

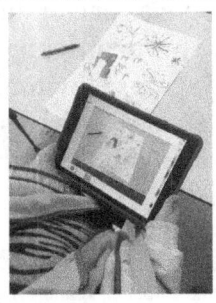 

Offering students a wide array of materials leads to more creativity during writing workshop. Students begin to tinker with different paper choices, various layouts and styles of presentation that match their learning style and voice. Offering students flexible seating options supports their innovation and individual needs for organization of materials. Creating opportunities for students to engage in gallery walks where they can discuss their own process and offer peer feedback leads to meaningful conversations around the revision process and next steps.

During reading workshop one day, I had a student who expressed that he was feeling angry with me. He told me that he wanted to use the materials from writing workshop during reading workshop, and he didn't understand why I put them away. He wanted to make, build, and record to support himself as a reader. He basically planned all of our mini lessons for the upcoming week. Students then transferred these skills to their word work lessons as well. It was such an incredible learning experience!

 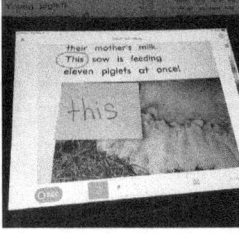  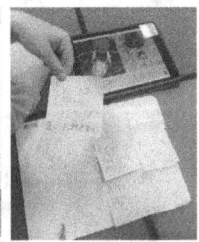

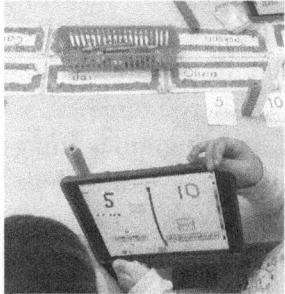

Why stop there? Can we use these same materials to represent our thinking during math workshop? Can we record ourselves discussing our thinking and learning? YES and YES! Turns out, we are writers and readers everywhere we go!

Having these materials available to students throughout the entirety of the school day created opportunities for them to have a voice in every area of their learning. Students recording their thinking and learning through audio gave me the opportunity to assess, reflect, and plan for next steps in our units.

How has multimodal composition moved beyond the walls of the kindergarten classroom?

After learning from kindergarteners for ten years, I now have the privilege of learning from students in grades K–4 as a Library Media Specialist. I have a unique opportunity to integrate multimodal composition experiences with inquiry and research across grade levels. Creating opportunities for students in grades K–4 to engage in activities where they determine their path for learning has empowered students and increased levels of engagement where they are exhibiting true ownership of their learning through multiple modes of expression. True equity lies within students having a voice in building their school community and having the tools to express themselves in ways that best support their individuality and unique strengths and abilities.

When considering entry points for all students to engage in modes of learning that best fit their needs, we are opening up avenues for learners, where there could otherwise be barriers. While students in grades 2–5 were embarking on our upcoming inquiry and research unit, we had discussions about frustrating barriers that get in the way of gathering research and taking notes. Students discussed note taking being too time consuming and the inability to write in books that are shared in the classroom or the library.

Copyright material from Stockman (2023), *The Writing Workshop Teacher's Guide to Multimodal Composition (K–5)*, Routledge.

We then discussed and experimented with ways to use the tools, resources, and materials around us to break down these barriers. Some students began taking pictures of texts with their devices and then using markup tools to jot down notes while they gathered research, while other students experimented with sketchnoting and drawing quick images, taking pictures of these notes, and recording themselves elaborating on their research, while others found it helpful to screenshot images from digital databases and voice record or use markup tools to gather their thinking and learning. This set up a strong foundation for students to engage in our inquiry and research unit.

To support the design thinking process, students are able to come to our library's makerspace to design prototypes, shop for materials to support their work in their classrooms, and experiment with various materials as they work to build, create, and innovate. To support this work, I've worked closely with other teachers to create cross curricular opportunities for students to extend their thinking and learning beyond the walls of their classrooms. Students use various modalities to support their own thinking, planning, making/building, and reflecting. These materials range from physical materials to digital tools. In the fall, our kindergarten students created plans to build pumpkins and gates to support their pumpkins. They recorded each step of their process with both physical and digital materials. To follow up on a 2D and 3D shape unit, our first graders were inspired by a famous artist who utilized shapes and colors to create his artwork and various books on buildings and architecture. First graders used this inspiration to design and create their own structures and then collaborated with a partner to join ideas and create a new design together. Our fourth grade students brainstormed ideas for a balloon and float parade. They felt inspired by various books, authors, and topics they had learned about across curricular areas, and each designed their own float or balloon to represent their learning. In each of these experiences, students are tinkering with process and product as they give and receive feedback and work through various iterations of their prototypes.

Andrea Schaber's Story ◆ 137

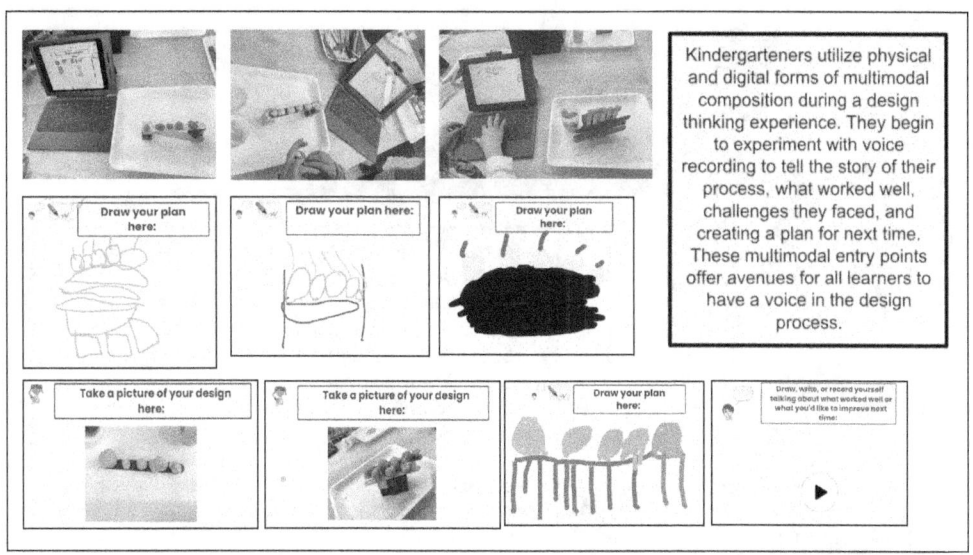

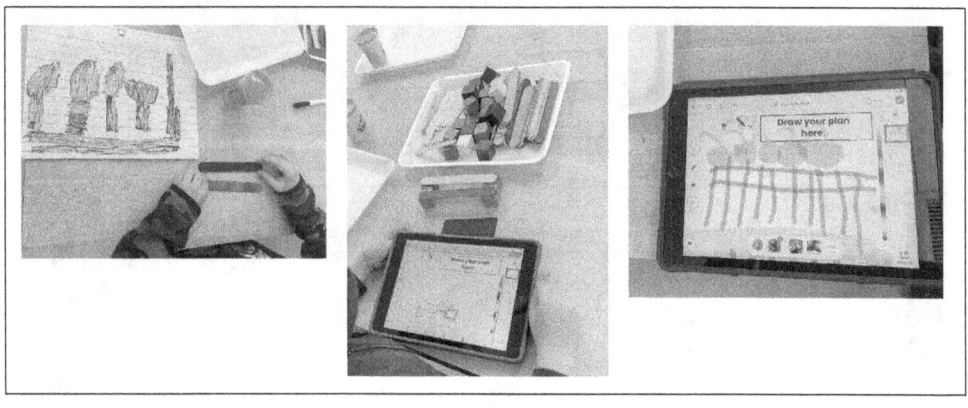

Copyright material from Stockman (2023), *The Writing Workshop Teacher's Guide to Multimodal Composition (K–5)*, Routledge.

Students in first grade felt inspired by a math unit when our art teacher introduced them to an artist who used shapes to design his masterpieces. Students explored various architecture and building design books while engaging in an independent shape inquiry. These shape-itects then partnered up for a collaborative project where they reflected, brainstormed, and designed a product together. This activity was topped off with a gallery walk and peer feedback! I learned so much from working with our art teacher and observing our students as designers. I am grateful for these collaborative experiences to view students through a different lens. So powerful!

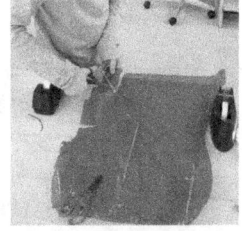

Students in fourth grade hosted a balloon and float parade for our school community to enjoy! They broke down the barriers between their classrooms and our makerspace as they utilized materials, tools, and resources in different capacities during their design process. Students thought about their intended audience and carefully chose characters, books, and curricular topics they felt passionate about to design prototypes to create their own floats and balloons for the parade. They demonstrated patience, flexibility, and determination as they worked to revise and finalize their projects. The process was simply remarkable!

Students rotate through stations around the library to engage in opportunities where they are encouraged to experiment with various types of materials and modes for gathering, processing, creating, and applying their thinking and learning to different forms of inquiry questions and research activities. One station requires students to reflect on themselves as researchers and determine which skills, tools, and strategies worked best for them while gathering and applying their research. This station also allows students to devise a plan for their next steps, and challenges them to devise a research plan with a different approach for their next station. It is my hope that students will feel confident in knowing about themselves as multimodal learners, feel empowered enough to transfer and apply these skills and strategies beyond the walls of our library, and share their voices, stories, and ideas with the world outside of our learning community.

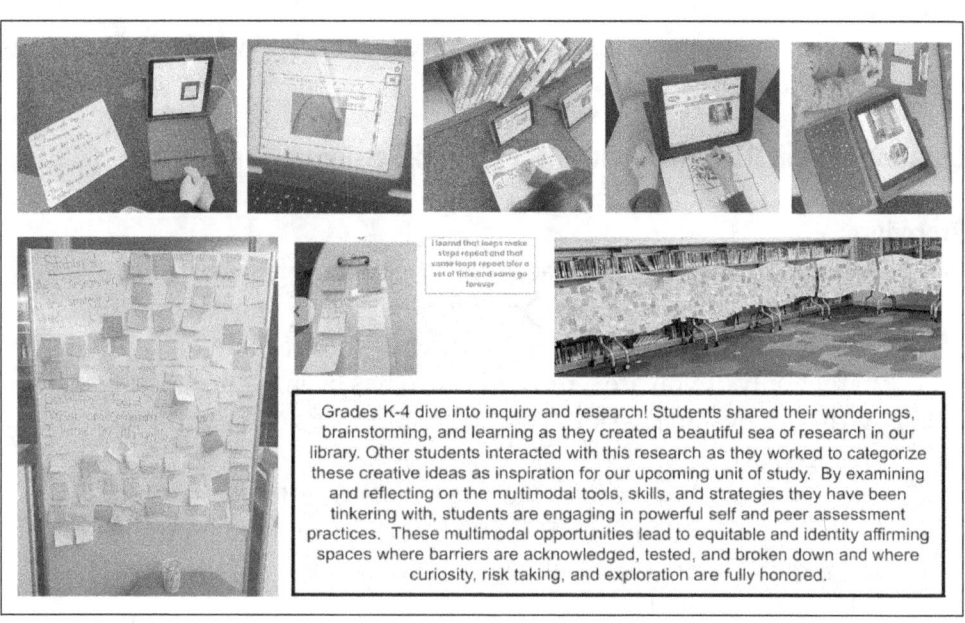

Grades K-4 dive into inquiry and research! Students shared their wonderings, brainstorming, and learning as they created a beautiful sea of research in our library. Other students interacted with this research as they worked to categorize these creative ideas as inspiration for our upcoming unit of study. By examining and reflecting on the multimodal tools, skills, and strategies they have been tinkering with, students are engaging in powerful self and peer assessment practices. These multimodal opportunities lead to equitable and identity affirming spaces where barriers are acknowledged, tested, and broken down and where curiosity, risk taking, and exploration are fully honored.

Feedback Structures, Protocols, and Frames for Writers and Designers

Structure: Over-the-Shoulder Feedback

Description:
This approach allows us to give high quality feedback to writers and designers quickly and consistently.

Duration of Typical Over-the-Shoulder Feedback Session: 1–2 minutes

Procedure:
1. What will your feedback address? If you are a teacher using over-the-shoulder feedback to reinforce what was taught during a lesson or conference, you may want to provide feedback on that specific target only. If you are a reviewer who has been approached by a writer or designer, ask what you should focus on as you frame your feedback.
2. Review a small portion of the work with your target in mind.
3. Offer warm feedback first: This is not a compliment but rather, an indication of specifically where progress toward the target has already been made.

   For example:
   "In the second paragraph, you use very precise words to describe the character's feelings."
   OR
   "Your font choice really carries the mood of this piece."

4. Offer only one bit of cool feedback next: This is not a criticism or a directive but rather, a question that invites critical thinking while respecting the creator's ownership of the work.

   For example:
   "How could you use precise word choice to show us how the character's mother feels in the third paragraph?"
   OR
   "What if you adjusted your camera angle in this shot? How might this shift perspective?"

5. Finally, offer but do not assign a specific approach that could move the work forward.

   For example:
   "The word sad hints at her feelings, but this kind of sad is very specific. Where could you find variations of the word sad in order to test them out?"
   OR
   "Using a wire frame might help you plan the home page and each of the subsequent landing pages of your site more efficiently. Try illustrating the user's touchpoints and where each will take them."

Structure: The Conference

Description:
Writing conferences are conducted between workshop participants and between single or small groups of participants and their teachers. They are held for a variety of purposes at a variety of times, but they're most often conducted once creators have become steeped in the process and reflective about their work. Writers and designers who consistently reflect on their work and review these reflections ahead of conferences often find the experience far more satisfying than those who don't. When you explore the structure of the traditional conference, you will understand why. I've provided some basic prompts and tools to support reflection on the pages that follow.

Duration of Typical Conference: 5–10 minutes

Procedure:
1. Prompt: Tell me about your work. How are things going?
2. Listen for important context about the process and the project.
3. Ask: How has your thinking, learning, or work changed?
4. Listen for important details about the learning that has occurred.
5. Ask: How might I help you?
6. Listen for a request for a specific kind of support.
7. Look into the work and ask additional clarifying questions.
8. Address the issue by providing the same type of warm and cool feedback you applied during your over-the-shoulder conversations.
9. Offer but don't assign specific strategies that might be considered to move the work forward.

An important note: During conferences, writers and designers often make important learning visible. Consider how you might document this learning. Whenever possible, invite them to document their learning themselves.

Protocol: Peer Review

Before you begin, divide the total amount of time provided for review by the number of writers or designers seeking feedback. This will help you determine how many minutes to devote to reviewing each person's work.

1. The writer/designer shares a selected piece or writing dilemma.
2. The writer/designer asks for specific feedback or a specific kind of support from the group.
3. Reviewers review the work carefully and independently.
4. Reviewers take up to five minutes to plan both warm and cool feedback.

Warm feedback is not a compliment. Consider the type of feedback requested and use evidence from the work to demonstrate where goals are already met or the writer/designer is demonstrating readiness to pursue them.

Cool feedback is not criticism. Consider the type of feedback requested and pose questions that may generate new ideas and solutions.

5. Reviewers share warm feedback first. They offer only *one* thought at a time, ensuring that all reviewers have an opportunity to contribute. When their feedback is exhausted, they may "pass." Once warm feedback rounds are complete, reviewers provide cool feedback in a similar fashion.
6. When peer review is complete, all work is returned to the writer/designer who chooses what, if any, feedback will be considered.
7. Reviews and writers/designers generate warm and cool feedback about the process and use it to define what they should stop/start/continue during the next review session.

Identifying Multimodal Learning Targets and Framing Meaningful Feedback

In Chapter 3, I introduced concepts for multimodal composition that will help you see your students' work in an informed way. Using them as lenses that help you see into multimodal compositions will add meaningful specificity to your warm and cool feedback. If this work is new to you, you may find the frames below useful. They're not comprehensive but instead, illustrative of how we *might* talk with writers and designers. As you become increasingly comfortable talking with writers and designers this way, you'll find your exchanges becoming less practiced and a bit more organic. That's a good thing.

Framing Warm Feedback	*Framing Cool Feedback*
Your use of x accomplishes y in this way . . .	If you did x instead of y, how might it accomplish z?
You made a good decision here. Choosing x really enhanced y.	What if you made a different choice here?
Changing x had this great effect on y.	How might changing x influence y?
You remembered what we learned about x, and this improved your work in this way . . .	Remember what we learned about x? How might you use it to revise y?
You chose an uncommon approach here, and I'm noticing this effect . . .	How might you tinker with x to innovate around y?
This seems to align with your purpose so well . . .	How might x create better alignment between y and z?
You juxtapose x and y nicely by choosing to do z.	How might you do x to juxtapose y and z?
Your audience is really going to appreciate . . .	Think about your intended audience? What might they appreciate here?
Here's what's most beneficial about your work . . .	Can you clarify this for me?
	Tell me more about z.
The combination of these things has this incredible result . . .	When I see x, it shows me you're ready to try y.
Your design/words are well structured here . . .	How might you use x to create the mood you're hoping for?
Your use of x establishes this specific mood . . .	How might you align x with y in order to best communicate your message?
Your message is carried best by these elements of your work.	How might you make x and y work together to accomplish z?
I love how x and y work together to accomplish z in this piece.	X seems to muddy y. What creative choices could you make to add more clarity instead?
X clarifies Y.	

Copyright material from Stockman (2023), *The Writing Workshop Teacher's Guide to Multimodal Composition (K–5)*, Routledge.

Five Ways to Explore Identity with Young Writers and Designers

1. **Create a Character Study:** Invite writers and designers to share their favorite characters from books, movies, animated shorts, comics, graphic novels, or other multimodal forms. Explicitly teach the concepts of identity, race, culture, gender, ethnicity, and ability, inviting students to use them as lenses to define the identities of their chosen characters. Challenge students to find classmates whose chosen characters share an identity with their own. Challenge them to find classmates whose chosen characters have very different identities as well. Then, offer these questions: Which characters do you most relate to? Why? Which ones do you feel you're very different from? Why? If you notice interesting similarities among all of the characters chosen, explore this with the class. What do all of these characters have in common? Why were they chosen? What could our character choices reveal about who we are?
2. **Feather Your Nest—Together:** As you come together to explore individual identities, invite your students to begin defining how your workshop or classroom might become a more welcoming and inclusive home to all of the writers and designers in your group. How might you work together to ensure that every student sees themselves inside of the books you read together, the videos you watch, the audio recordings you listen to, the materials you make and write with, the posters, charts, and decorations you use with the space, and the celebrations you enjoy together? Seek feedback from your students. They may notice much about representation that you don't. They may also be willing and eager to add books, illustrations, multimedia resources, or other artifacts to your workshop environment.
3. **Create a Notebook Cover:** Encourage writers to design notebook covers that reflect the things about their identities that give them the most pride.
4. **Identify Mentors:** Invite writers and designers to learn more about famous writers and designers who share their identities. Elevate their work, use what they've created as models for what your students might write and make, and notice when your students do things that remind you of these experts and their work. Point it out to them. Validate their efforts.
5. **The Best Parts of Us:** Once students are more aware of how identity is shaped and what the elements of their own identities are, invite them

to define the aspects of their identities that they feel are their greatest strengths or points of pride. Invite them to think about classmates whose identities may be slightly or even dramatically different from their own. Ask them to define the aspects of their classmate's identity that they feel are most wonderful. Encourage them to share and then, encourage them to compare the strengths they identified in themselves to those that their classmates shared about them.

Appendix B

Tools for Writers

Mentor Text Sources and Tools for Young Writers and Designers

Crowdsourced by the Building Better Writers Facebook Group, facilitated by Angela Stockman

I want to make:	*Mentor texts and tools that might help me:*
A multimodal recipe card, book, video, or site	Hoopla Recipes (https://www.youtube.com/channel/UC-vObULK1w635bdFQpNlbQA) Taste of Home: 30 Recipes Kids Can Make on Their Own (tasteofhome.com) Raddish Kids RadTV Cooking Videos (https://www.raddishkids.com/blogs/bonus-bites/tagged/facebook-live-videos) Nomster Chef (https://www.nomsterchef.com/) Cooking with Kids (https://cookingwithkids.org/) Canva (https://www.canva.com)
A funny video or a stop motion video	The Comedy Rule of Three (https://youtu.be/s2lgdrAgmZY) Animotica (https://www.animotica.com/) Magistro (https://www.magisto.com/) Animoto (https://animoto.com/) Filmora (https://filmora.wondershare.net) Toontastic (https://toontastic.withgoogle.com)

(Continued)

I want to make:	Mentor texts and tools that might help me:
	Clips (https://www.apple.com/clips/)
	Adobe Spark Video (https://spark.adobe.com/make/video-maker/)
	We Video (https://www.wevideo.com/)
	OSnap! (https://www.osnapphotoapp.com/)
	Chatterpix (http://chatterpix/)
	Do Ink (http://www.doink.com/)
	Draw and Tell (https://apps.apple.com/us/app/draw-and-tell/id504750621)
	Stop Motion Animation (A Guide for Kids) (https://play.google.com/store/apps/details?id=com.Stop.Motion.Animation.Movie.Maker)
	Stop Motion Cartoon Maker (https://play.google.com/store/apps/details?id=com.whisperarts.kids.stopmotion)
	Stickbot Studio (https://play.google.com/store/apps/details?id=com.zingglobal.stikbot2&hl=en_IN&gl=US)
	Play-Doh Stop Motion Videos (https://steprimo.com/android/us/app/com.playdohstopmotion.video42/Play-Doh-Stop-Motion-Videos/)

I want to make:	Mentor texts and tools that might help me:
An infographic	Infographic Tools for Kids (https://www.coolcatteacher.com/infographic-tools-for-kids/)
	Visme (https://www.visme.co/)
	Snappa (https://snappa.com/)
	Animaker (https://www.animaker.com/infographics)
	PicMonkey (https://www.picmonkey.com/)
	Canva (https://www.canva.com)
	Venngage (https://venngage.com/)
	Piktochart (https://piktochart.com/)
	easel.ly (https://www.easel.ly/)
	BeFunky (https://www.befunky.com/)
	Biteable (https://biteable.com/infographic/)
	MindTheGraph (https://mindthegraph.com/)
A pamphlet, flier, poster, brochure, newsletter, business cards	5 Graphic Design Projects Kids Will Love (https://www.learningliftoff.com/5-graphic-design-projects-and-games/#.WP9KqjsrJEZ)
	Canva (https://www.canva.com)
	KidPix (https://www.mackiev.com/kidpix)
	TuxPaint (https://tuxpaint.org)
	Adobe Spark Flyer (https://www.adobe.com/express/create/flyer)

(*Continued*)

I want to make:	*Mentor texts and tools that might help me:*
A meme	Tips for Making Hilarious Memes (https://www.picmonkey.com/blog/tips-for-making-hilarious-memes)
	Three Tools for Making Memes in School (https://bit.ly/3tLx0QB)
	Meme Generation in Google Drawings (https://bit.ly/3Cx8jLG)
	IMGFlip (https://imgflip.com/memegenerator)
	Photo Director (https://www.cyberlink.com/products/apps/photodirector_en_US.html)
A song	The Best Music Apps for Kids (https://www.bestappsforkids.com/2017/best-music-apps-for-kids/)
	Figure (https://apps.apple.com/us/app/figure-make-music-beats/id511269223)
	Classics for Kids (https://www.classicsforkids.com/games/compose_your_own_music.php)
	BandLab (https://www.bandlab.com/)
	n-Track Studio l DAW (https://apps.apple.com/gb/app/n-track-studio-daw-9/id1130289718)
	GarageBand (https://apps.apple.com/us/app/garageband/id408709785)
	Suggester (https://apps.apple.com/us/app/suggester/id504740787)
	Groovebox (https://apps.apple.com/us/app/groovebox/id1242847278)
	Beat Maker Go (https://apps.apple.com/us/app/beat-maker-go-make-music/id1141835258)

I want to make:	*Mentor texts and tools that might help me:*
A craft	The DIY Network (https://www.diynetwork.com/how-to/packages/rainy-day-diy-craft-projects-for-kids) The Best Ideas for Kids (https://bit.ly/36a7IDE) Instructable Crafts (https://www.instructables.com/craft/)
Art	Free Online Drawing Lessons Led by Favorite Illustrators (http://www.openculture.com/2020/03/free-online-drawing-lessons-for-kids-led-by-favorite-artists-illustrators.html) Deep Space Sparkle (https://www.deepspacesparkle.com/category/art-lessons/) Videos (https://www.youtube.com/channel/UCYL_pWOSf1FnQSwF11T-vBw) Instructables (https://www.instructables.com/craft/art/projects/) Pixelart (https://www.pixilart.com/draw)
A television show	How a TV Show Gets Made (https://www.youtube.com/watch?v=P8aW1Ae6gcI) Animotica (https://www.animotica.com/) Magistro (https://www.magisto.com/) Animoto (https://animoto.com/) Filmora (https://filmora.wondershare.net) Toontastic (https://toontastic.withgoogle.com) Clips (https://www.apple.com/clips/) Adobe Spark Video (https://spark.adobe.com/make/video-maker/) We Video (https://www.wevideo.com/)

(*Continued*)

I want to make:	*Mentor texts and tools that might help me:*
An experiment	Kids' DIY Craft Activities (https://www.kiwico.com/diy) Exploratorium (https://www.exploratorium.edu/) Science Bob (https://sciencebob.com/) PHET Colorado (https://phet.colorado.edu/en/simulations/category/by-level/elementary-school) Steve Spangler Science Experiments (https://www.stevespanglerscience.com/lab/)
A sport	A Maker Challenge from John Spencer (https://youtu.be/rLKa2weeajI) Invent a Sport on Instructables (https://www.instructables.com/id/Invent-a-Sport-1/)
An escape room	Symbaloo (https://edu.symbaloo.com/) BreakoutEdu (https://breakoutedu.com/) 40+ Free Digital Escape Rooms and a How-To Guide (https://ditchthattextbook.com/30-digital-escape-rooms-plus-tips-and-tools-for-creating-your-own/)
A board game	Board Games on Instructables (https://www.instructables.com/howto/a+board+game/) WikiHow to Make Your Own Board Game (https://www.wikihow.com/Make-Your-Own-Board-Game) Create Your Own Board Game: PBS Kids (https://www.pbs.org/parents/crafts-and-experiments/create-your-own-board-game)

I want to make:	Mentor texts and tools that might help me:
An app-based game	Hopscotch (https://www.gethopscotch.com/)
	ScratchJr (https://www.scratchjr.org)
A story or novel	NaNoWriMo Workbook (https://bit.ly/3KA9ZGX)
	Writing Prompts from John Spencer (https://www.youtube.com/results?search_query=john+spencer+story+writing)
	MyStoryBook (https://www.mystorybook.com/)
A poem	Amy Ludwig Vanderwater's Poem Farm (http://www.poemfarm.amylv.com/)
	Poem Generator (https://www.poem-generator.org.uk/)
	Poetry Generator (https://www.poemofquotes.com/tools/poetry-generator/)
	Bored Humans AI Poetry Generator (https://boredhumans.com/poetry_generator.php)
	Poetry Games (https://www.poetrygames.org/)
	Metaphor Dice (https://www.metaphordice.com/)
A podcast	Starting Your Own Podcast: A Guide for Students (https://www.npr.org/2018/11/15/662070097/starting-your-podcast-a-guide-for-students)
	Anchor (https://anchor.fm/)
	PodBean (https://www.podbean.com/)
Solutions by coding	MinecraftEdu (https://education.minecraft.net/)

(*Continued*)

Copyright material from Stockman (2023), *The Writing Workshop Teacher's Guide to Multimodal Composition (K–5)*, Routledge.

I want to make:	Mentor texts and tools that might help me:
Photography	Teaching Kids Photo-Editing (https://www.picmonkey.com/blog/teaching-kids-photo-editing)
	The Best Photo-Editing Apps for Kids (https://www.commonsense.org/education/top-picks/best-photography-and-photo-editing-apps-for-students)
A garden	Ideas on Instructables (https://www.instructables.com/howto/gardening/)
3D object	Tinkercad (https://www.tinkercad.com/)
Animated shorts	The Kids Should See This (https://thekidshouldseethis.com/)

Multimodal Mentor Texts

The texts below are organized by the modes that are most primary to each. All are multimodal compositions that rely on various modes of expression. Some are intended to inform and inspire you as a creative teacher. Others are especially appropriate for children to explore.

Notably Visual

Look
(https://www.nytimes.com/column/magazine-look)

Once Upon a Picture
(https://www.onceuponapicture.co.uk/the-collections/the-character-collection/)

Animagraffs: Animated Inforgraphics
(https://animagraffs.com/)

10 Photo Stories That Will Challenge Your View of the World
(https://www.buzzfeednews.com/article/gabrielsanchez/photo-stories-april-5-news-trending-art-photograph)

David M. Bird: Photo Stories
(https://www.instagram.com/davidmbird/)

Stories Worth Seeing
(https://medium.com/stories-worth-seeing/a-new-medium-on-medium-9e4b085efe25)

Tween Tribune
(https://www.tweentribune.com/)

Winter 2022 Virtual Book Room
(https://padlet.com/clare_landrigan/y4vrm5bp5lcvufq0)

Morphing Gifs
(https://www.huffpost.com/entry/the-eye-opening-evolution-of-miss-americas-body-over-95-years_n_55f078d9e4b002d5c077a6fb)

Riding the Silk
(https://www.nytimes.com/newsgraphics/2013/07/21/silk-road/index.html)

Copyright material from Stockman (2023), *The Writing Workshop Teacher's Guide to Multimodal Composition (K–5)*, Routledge.

The Deep Fake
(https://www.theguardian.com/technology/ng-interactive/2019/jun/22/the-rise-of-the-deepfake-and-the-threat-to-democracy)

Notably Aural

NPR Audio News Stories
(https://www.npr.org/sections/news/)

The Ringer Podcast Network
(https://www.theringer.com/pages/podcasts)

Tai Asks Why
(https://www.cbc.ca/radio/taiaskswhy)

Radioactive
(https://www.kuow.org/radioactive)

The Bench Racing Podcast
(https://podcasts.apple.com/us/podcast/the-bench-racing-podcast/id1497189157)

Tiny Circus: The Art Classroom
(https://youtu.be/yIs4VmEkyGk)

Language and Spending
(https://youtu.be/S3G51gDHTXE)

Google Arts and Culture: Play with Music and Sound
https://artsandculture.google.com/project/games

Notably Spatial

Graphic Novels and Comics
(https://guides.nyu.edu/graphic-novels/journals)

Daily Infographic
(https://www.dailyinfographic.com/)

Delayed Gratification
(https://www.slow-journalism.com/blog)

Go Comics
(https://www.gocomics.com/)

E-Graphic Novel Recommendations for All Ages
(https://www.nypl.org/blog/2020/04/24/e-graphic-novels-all-ages)

Stand Up Tall: Stop Motion Video
(https://youtu.be/PkALQS-OjZQ)

Perceptions of Perfect Men
(https://onlinedoctor.superdrug.com/perceptions-of-perfection-part-ii-men/)

Scientology's Clear Takeover
(https://projects.tampabay.com/projects/2019/investigations/scientology-clearwater-real-estate/)

Scaling Mt. Everest
(https://www.washingtonpost.com/graphics/world/scaling-everest/)

Notably Gestural

Button Poetry
(https://buttonpoetry.com/category/videos/)

Pexels Royalty Free Videos
(https://www.pexels.com/videos/)

Merce Cunningham Trust Viewing Room
(https://www.mercecunningham.org/)

Improv for Kids
(https://www.youtube.com/channel/UCF6TEGdFdeD3_L4W2ptLX2g)

Student Stop Motion Videos: PBS
(https://ny.pbslearningmedia.org/resource/media_arts_classroom8/student-stop-motion-animations/)

Notably Haptic

10 Most Interesting Ways Games Have Used Controller Vibration
(https://www.cbr.com/video-games-best-vibration-usage/)

The Haptic Stack—Design Layer
(https://www.immersion.com/the-haptic-stack-design-layer/)

Copyright material from Stockman (2023), *The Writing Workshop Teacher's Guide to Multimodal Composition (K–5)*, Routledge.

The Neuroscience of Touch
(https://www.sappi.com/the-neuroscience-of-touch)

Haptics: 6 Reasons Touch Is Important
(https://www.ultraleap.com/company/news/blog/haptics-touch-important/)

Ink Stories
(https://inkstories.com/)

Notably Alphabetic

Lit Hub
(https://lithub.com/)

The New York Times Learning Network
(https://www.nytimes.com/column/learning-mentor-texts)

Slate
(https://slate.com/)

The Atlantic
(https://www.theatlantic.com/)

Vulture
(https://www.vulture.com/)

Storyline Online
(https://storylineonline.net/)

International Children's Digital Library
(http://en.childrenslibrary.org/)

Library of Congress: Read.gov
(https://read.gov/kids/)

Oxford Owl
(https://www.oxfordowl.co.uk/)

Publishing Opportunities for Young Writers and Designers

This site lists markets, contests, and virtual communities for young writers and designers: https://www.livebinders.com/b/18928

Starter Sets

1. The Stop Motion Starter Set: https://bit.ly/3I3oOQK
2. Layered Storyboarding: https://bit.ly/3i0xHQo
3. The Make Writing Starter Set: https://bit.ly/3Jby8DG